Art Projects Middle Schoolers Can't Resist!

by Bernard Winter

NEW YORK • TORONTO • LONDON • AUCKLAND • SYDNEY
MEXICO CITY • NEW DELHI • HONG KONG • BUENOS AIRES

SCHOLASTIC
Teaching
Resources

This book is dedicated to kids everywhere who want to make something cool.

ACKNOWLEDGMENTS

I am grateful for the assistance of specialist teachers from the Mario Salvadori Middle School Program for Architectural Design in New York. The program teaches middle-school students basic concepts in architectural design through hands-on projects and experimentation. Its teachers provided valuable help in developing the Sky's the Limit: Skyscraper Contest project.

I also wish to acknowledge the talented students from Middle School 222 in the Bronx, New York, for their contributions of their artwork as examples through-out the book. Many thanks to Eric, Maritza, Louisa, Kinanhi, Nelson, Melissa, Paola, Rasheed, and Jonathan for being good sports.

Cover design by Solás Design
Cover art by Jason Robinson
Interior design by Solutions by Design, Inc.
Interior illustration by Bernard Winter

ISBN: 0-439-44409-8

2 3 4 5 6 7 8 9 10   40   09 08 07 06 05 04 03

Contents

Introduction

I HAD TAUGHT ART IN NEW YORK CITY AT THE ELEMENTARY SCHOOL LEVEL FOR twelve years when I was transferred to a middle school in 1999. Suddenly, the extensive repertory of art projects I had used to teach kindergarten through fourth grade students was greeted with flat statements of disapproval. "This is boring... we've done this before!" my students told me. They were right—and sheer necessity forced me to adjust my curriculum to meet my students' needs and interests. The projects I developed from my middle school experience form the core of this book and each project is kid tested and kid approved.

If you've taught grades 5 through 8, you know that the middle-school years are a time of accelerating growth, change, and instability. A boy or girl in these grades is fundamentally different from a sibling in second or third grade. Middle-school students are generally more active, more opinionated, more peer oriented, and more socially needy than younger children. They like to work together, plan, argue, discuss, and delegate. Their fine motor skills are well developed, and they find satisfaction in completing intricate work. Middle schoolers also enjoy complex projects that take planning and multiple steps. I've found that they often express a strong desire to build something in collaboration that expresses higher aspirations and makes significant statements. In fact, the seeds of a future career are often developed in these years. The pleasure that a young person takes in mastering an art or design project can nourish a future architect, engineer, painter, or fashion designer.

Too often, middle-school students have limited opportunities to experience creating art. Art has become an elective in some schools and many design course options limit students' hands-on experience with materials. The projects in this book integrate that irreplaceable kind of learning that occurs when a student learns how to measure, cut, assemble, and organize materials—learning which cannot be duplicated by a student knowing how to use a command key.

Making time for project-based learning in the middle-school curriculum is a challenge, but one that is well worth the effort. Art projects within the curriculum allow for each student to respond to what they learn with their own personal voice, and art projects can hold the attention of academically "at risk" and special needs learners. You'll find projects within this book that cross over and connect curriculum areas—science, math, history, creative writing—within the context of a meaningful art project.

If you teach in a self-contained class, look over your schedule to find the most natural place to schedule project time. Once they get going, kids won't want to stop, so consider scheduling a double period. Much more progress will be accomplished in one double period than in two discrete art periods.

I hope that these projects will so engage students that they'll look up and say, "Aw, gee, is the period over?" Isn't that the experience we all hope to have?

Let's create!
Bernard Winter

How to Use This Book

The projects in this book are organized around three big themes: "Portraits of Myself," "Patterns Around Us," and "Designing Our World." Projects within each theme can be done sequentially or independently. Each project is planned to be easy and accessible to the majority of students' abilities. No extraordinary art materials are involved, only commonly available materials, such as manila folders, index cards, and colored pencils are used. You can complete each project without painting or getting your hands messy—making it ideal for the classroom teacher who is looking to enrich their curriculum without going overboard on extensive cleanups.

Each lesson follows the same format. Additionally, throughout the book, the following features can be of great help to you:

✹ **Tips:** bright ideas that will smooth out the process for you

✹ **How-To Page:** a full-page reproducible showing steps for construction

✹ **Project Parameters Page:** a full-page reproducible with specific parameters to be followed

✹ **Drawing/Coloring Reproducible:** a full-page reproducible to distribute to students for drawing to plan ideas

✹ **Photographs of Finished Projects:** give you an idea how the project might look

This book concludes with a student evaluation reproducible on page 80. Copy and distribute this page at the conclusion of any project to help students reflect on their learning and internalize new strategies they may have used.

National K–12 Visual Arts Standards

The following standards for the visual arts were used in developing these lessons. Other national curriculum standards are cited as they apply in individual lessons.

The student:

1. Understands and applies media, techniques, and processes related to the visual arts.

2. Knows how to use structures (sensory qualities, organizational principles, expressive features) and functions of art.

3. Knows a range of subject matter, symbols, and potential ideas in the visual arts.

4. Understands the visual arts in relation to history and cultures.

5. Understands the characteristics and merits of one's own artwork and the artwork of others.

Managing Art Activities in the Classroom

The best advice I can give to teachers who want to use this project book, or any other project book, is to try out the project first. The process of creating the project will clarify many questions you may have. You can also assess whether the project is age appropriate and can challenge students' skill levels without frustrating them. You can find out which point in the project might call for a mini-lesson (such as measuring with the quarter inch scale of the ruler). You can gauge how many periods it might take your class to work on and finish the project. Finally, you can assess whether the project would really hold your students' interest. A good rule of thumb: If you enjoyed making the project, in all likelihood, they will too.

Use the project you create as an example for students. Talk about your personal experience in creating the project, what you liked about it, and what you discovered.

It is often helpful in multiple-step projects to have more than one model available, each at a different level of completion, so that the steps in assembling the project are clearly seen. For example, I would demonstrate the maze project (pages 57–62) by having the following models available:

* example of the grid to be measured

* example of the grid with the perimeter, entrance, and exit completed

* a few constructed barriers, to show how they can be arranged within the perimeter

* the finished maze, so you can drop a marble inside and have students try it out

In addition to models, charts showing step-by-step procedures are a great help. For this purpose, the "How-To" reproducible pages show construction step by step. You can either make copies for each student or place the reproducible on an overhead projector so the entire class can see your explanation.

Tips for Time and Cleanup

Time management is crucial in the art room. Sometimes we get caught up in creating the project and forget that it's time for lunch or look up and see our next class at the door! Here are some survival tips for time and cleanup:

1 *Use a clock or a timer. Set the timer to give the class a reminder five minutes before they should stop. Then re-set the timer so it goes off when the class should stop.*

2 *Since art periods tend to be noisy, use a visual or auditory signal to get the class to stop, look, and listen. Practice stopping art activities with your class!*

3 *Create and post a job chart. Who will collect the projects and store them? Who will wipe up tables and who will pick up paper scraps? If you are an arts specialist, number your seats 1 to 4 or 1 to 6. When it's time to clean up, students will look at the chart to find their number listed next to a job. All the number 1s will put away projects, while all the number 2s will pick up paper scraps, and so forth.*

4 *If you use paint, put paint into paper cups, which students can hold onto while painting. You might even have pre-mixed colors available. When students finish with a color, they may return it to the front of the room, making a color lending library.*

5 *If you don't have a sink in your room, or wish to avoid a crowd at your sink, use disposable pre-moistened baby wipes for students to use to clean up their hands. They work!*

"Who am I?" Pop-Up Riddle Book

Create a pop-up book that reveals each student's personality, hopes, and dreams

Pop-up books are easy to make but contain an element of surprise, too. This project and its variations provide a fun way for students to get to know each other at the beginning of the year. Students are always eager to see and show pictures of friends and classmates, so this project is a sure crowd pleaser!

What Students Will Learn and Do

- ☀ Create a pop-up book about themselves.
- ☀ Write hints that describe their appearance and personality.
- ☀ Revise their writing to clarify or make their hints more effective.
- ☀ Learn to organize factual material and details.

Materials

How to Create a Pop-Up Book reproducible, page 12

Legal-size manila folders, cut in half to make 7" × 8" booklets, one per student

STANDARDS

Visual Arts

Standard 1: Understands and applies media, techniques, and processes related to the visual arts.

English Language Arts

Standard 5: Uses a wide range of strategies as he/she writes and uses different writing process elements appropriately to communicate with different audiences and for different purposes.

Standard 12: Uses spoken, written, and visual language to accomplish his/her own purposes (for learning, enjoyment, persuasion, and the exchange of information).

Pictures of students

Scissors, rulers, glue sticks or tape

Colored pencils or magic markers

Get the Class Thinking

Make a pop-up riddle book about yourself, following the steps below. Read the hints on the front cover, pause, and then read the three hints on the back. Ask the class if they can guess who this is. Open the booklet, show the picture of yourself and reveal your "secret wish." Explain that each student will make a pop-up riddle book to share with the class.

Getting Started

 Take pictures of your students, or have them bring in a photo from home. You may want to do this a week before you begin.

Tips: ❶ *An inexpensive digital camera is a great help in photographing students, and you can purchase one for under $100. Digital photographs save money in the long run on film, developing, and printing costs.*

❷ *Remember that many adolescents are shy about their appearance and may be embarrassed to be photographed in front of the whole class. Take photos of these students in small groups of friends during your prep period.*

 It's writing time! Have students write a draft of their hints. Tell them to keep these hints a secret as much as possible. The following is a basic list of hints, appropriate for younger students:

Hints: Front cover

1. Write a hint about how you look.

2. Write a hint about something that you are good at.

3. Write a hint about your personality.

Hints: Back cover

1. Write another hint about how you look.

2. Write a hint about your family.

3. Write a hint about your best friend, but don't use your best friend's name.

Inside: Top

Surprise! It's me! My name is: _____

Inside: Bottom

My secret wish is: _____

(Write about something you want to do or be that you are ready to tell us about.)

Assure the class that the "secret wish" they reveal on the inside is something that they choose to share with the class at this time. Don't force any revelation to be made that a student is not comfortable sharing. A variation on the "secret wish" may be "I've always wanted to…" or "My dream for my future is…" or "My greatest strength is…"

Tip: *Make variations on the hints, as the kind of hints you propose can be a prompt for more creative writing. Try some of these or brainstorm new ones with your class:*

> *"Something I look forward to every day is…"*
> *"My biggest pet peeve is…"*
> *"I feel proud about…"*
> *"My favorite food is…"*
> *"My hero is…"*
> *"I can't stand it when…"*

Let's Create!

1 **Distribute the manila folder booklets.**

2 **Create the pop-up box.** Have students follow these steps:

See How to Create Your Pop-Up Book (page 12) for visual instructions.

1. Draw two parallel lines in the middle of the spine of the booklet (one on either side of the center fold), 1" to $1\frac{1}{2}$" deep, and $2\frac{1}{2}$" inches apart. Use the side of a cassette box to help mark these lines.

2. Cut the two parallel lines with a scissor. Take care that the lines are the same length. Open the booklet. Insert your two thumbs and press down to form a crease.

3. Close the booklet, press down, and crease.

3 **Have students use rulers to draw parallel lines (1" apart)** to guide their writing on the front, back, and inside.

4 **Write out hints on the booklets.** Review with students what makes a good hint, and have them revise any hints that are too obvious or confusing.

Finish the Project

5 **Add the photograph** by taping or gluing the photo to the pop-up box as shown in the diagram on page 12.

6 **Add color and decorations** with markers or pencils.

7 **Play the game.** Collect all the booklets. Shuffle them and then redistribute so that students will read someone else's booklet. Have students take turns reading the hints to the class, and allow the class to guess after they hear the first three hints on the front cover. If the class needs additional clues, have the clue reader continue reading on the back cover, let students take another guess, and then open to reveal whom it is!

Display It!

This project makes a great bulletin board for the beginning of the year. It integrates perfectly with "All About Me" themes, which start the year off for many teachers. Staple the booklets so that the "Who Am I?" cover shows and can be lifted to reveal the photograph.

Art and Language Extensions

- Try combining the pop-up book with the idea of shaped books, such as books in the shape of a heart or star.
- Try variations on the book. Since the pop-up is also a riddle book, use the power of riddles to intrigue students in reviewing material in any content area:

Social Studies: Ask students to write "Who Am I?" pop-up books presenting facts as hints about the presidents of the United States, African-American heroes, famous women authors, etc. Instead of a "secret wish" the inside may contain a picture with information such as an individual's greatest accomplishment.

Science: Challenge students to write "What Am I?" pop-up books to review facts about the solar system, organs of the body, animals of the rain forest, the periodic table, or other topics. Have students write the most amazing fact about their topic on the inside of the book and include a picture.

Language Arts: Create more riddle books by having students clip pictures from magazines and write hints about everyday objects. Avoid obvious hints by not disclosing what the object is used for.

Investigate Further

Invite students who enjoy creating pop-up books to investigate how to create complicated pop-ups found in the books listed below.

Book Links

The Pop-Up Book: Step-by-Step Instructions for Creating Over 100 Original Paper Projects by Paul Jackson and Paul Forrester (Owl Books, New York, 1994)

The Elements of Pop-Up: A Pop-Up Book for Aspiring Paper Engineers by David Carter and James Diaz (Simon & Schuster, 1999)

EVALUATE THE PROJECT

1. The student created a pop-up book with hints and a picture inside.

     1   **2**   **3**   **4**

2. The student's hints were well written, neither too obvious nor too confusing.

     1   **2**   **3**   **4**

3. The student's decorations added to the uniqueness of the project.

     1   **2**   **3**   **4**

EXTENSION EVALUATIONS

1. The student's pop-up book about a historical personality or an object contains accurate facts that are well sequenced.

     1   **2**   **3**   **4**

(Scale of 1 to 4; 4 indicates mastery, 1 indicates a lack of comprehension or achievement)

How to Create a Pop-Up Book

Measure lines to cut along fold.

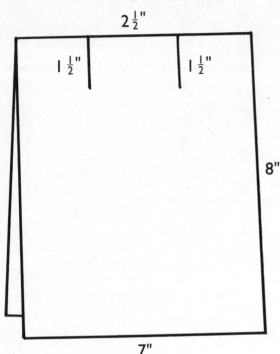

$2\frac{1}{2}$"

$1\frac{1}{2}$" $1\frac{1}{2}$"

8"

7"

Push open box.

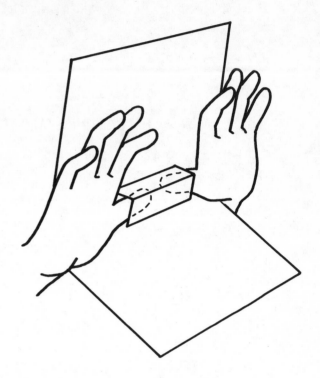

Close and crease. Rule guide lines for writing on front, inside, and back.

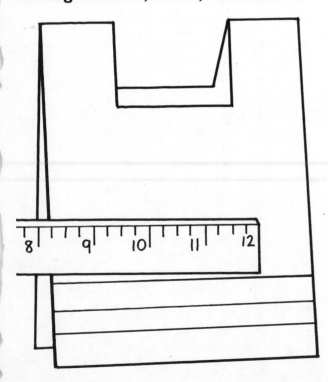

Add photograph or drawing with glue or tape.

SURPRISE! IT'S ME!

MY SECRET WISH

That's Me: Paper Self-Portraits

Create a paper self-portrait using collage techniques

Self-portraiture always holds students' interest, and variations on this project will challenge older students to use their increasing level of skill in representation. Beginning with basic shapes, students will add features to build a likeness that also conveys a feeling or expression. Finally—something good you can do with those packs of construction paper in your closet!

What Students Will Learn and Do

- ☀ Create a paper self-portrait.
- ☀ Experiment with collage techniques.
- ☀ Create two-dimensional and three-dimensional paper shapes.
- ☀ Learn about the basic proportions of the human face.
- ☀ Experiment with placement and exaggeration of features to create expressions.

Materials

A variety of colored construction paper, 12" x 18"

Colored paper in shades of brown for a variety of skin tones

How to Create a Self-Portrait reproducible, pages 19–20

Gift wrap paper, sections of wall paper, magazines

Gold or silver gift wrap paper

STANDARDS

Visual Arts

Standard 1: Understands and applies media, techniques, and processes related to the visual arts.

Standard 2: Knows how to use structures (sensory qualities, organizational principles, expressive features) and functions of art.

Standard 4: Understands the visual arts in relation to history and cultures.

Math: Geometry

Standard 1: Analyzes characteristics and properties of two- and three-dimensional shapes.

White glue or glue sticks

Scissors, rulers, pencils

White drawing paper

9" diameter paper plates

Paper cups, pennies, standard letter envelopes

Colored pencils, markers, crayons

Handheld mirrors

Get the Class Thinking

Portraits convey feeling as well as information about a person. Show examples of portraits in a variety of media with strong personalities, moods, or features. Challenge students to analyze why someone in a portrait may look disappointed, hopeful, or bored. What are the eyebrows doing? Does the mouth smile or frown? Do the eyes look directly at you or are they looking off to the side? Have mirrors handy; encourage your students to make facial expressions and notice how the position of certain features universally correspond to certain emotions.

Distinguish between a portrait and a self-portrait. Show a self-portrait you've made and talk about the process you followed to create it, the expression you were after, and the decisions you made about shapes and placement.

Getting Started

1 **Select three pieces of 12" x 18" construction paper;** one sheet for the background, one sheet for a shirt color, one sheet for a skin color.

> **Tips:** ❶ *Construction papers are now made in "multi-cultural packs," with a greater range of browns to approximate skin tones. Brown wrapping paper, paper bags, and school "newsprint" paper will also work with this project.*
>
> ❷ *Some students may want to pick a pink paper or another color much lighter than their real skin tone. Suggest that they place the construction paper next to their forearm to find the closest match. Positive statements such as "Here's a beautiful brown for you" can go a long way to help a reluctant student to accept his or her own natural beauty.*

See How to Create a Self-Portrait (pages 19–20) for visual instructions.

2 **Trace a 9" paper plate on skin-colored paper to create a basic head shape.** Paper plates work well for young children whose heads are very round. Older students might want to trim the circle shape into an oval. To do this, have them fold the circle in half and trim off a fingernail shaped sliver. Unfold and flatten out.

3 **Measure and cut out a 5" square for the neck.** Make sure that the skin color students choose matches that of the head.

4 **Measure and cut out a rectangle for the shirt.** Ask students to use a ruler or approximate a rectangle with dimensions that range between 6" x 8" to 7" x 10". The top corners of the rectangle can be rounded off to create shoulders.

5 **Position the head, neck, and shirt onto the background paper.** Have students place the rectangle of the shirt on the bottom edge of the background paper, tuck the square neck under the rectangle, and glue the pieces down. Then have them glue the circle or oval for the head on top of the neck, allowing some of the neck to show.

Let's Create!

Up to now, all the self-portraits should look very similar. With the next steps, students will diversify their process to create unique features and personalities. Details added to the portrait in the foreground and background will provide a sense of texture and layering.

1 **Create the background.** The background puts the portrait in a context and provides information about the person in the portrait. There are many options for the background:

  ✳ Make a collage of magazine pictures that relate to students' interests and hobbies.

  ✳ Use gift wrap paper to add colors and patterns.

  ✳ Create a mosaic-like texture using cut paper squares (approximately 1") in alternating colors.

2 **Personalize the shirt.** Ask students to examine a favorite shirt and use construction paper to create buttons, collars, and pockets. Then have them apply gift wrap to the shirt to add patterns and color. Gold or silver gift wrap, or aluminum foil can be used to create jewelry.

3 **Create the frame of the face.** The basic proportions of the face are included in the handout to students. Photocopy this page for each student to use while they are working. Distribute hand held mirrors. Students should add the features in the following sequence:

  a) Ears: Using paper that matches the skin color, have students trace around the rim of the cup to create a circle, fold, and cut in half. Since the ears have the basic shape of half a heart rather than a half circle, have them trim and adjust. Using the analogy of the clock face, they should position the ears at the 9:00 and 3:00 position. Glue down, tucking them under the circle or oval face if possible.

  Tip: *Ears are an important guide to the structure of the face; the eyes will line up along the horizontal line created by the top of the ears. Don't forget earrings!*

  b) Hair: Select an appropriate color for the hair. Using the paper plate as a template, ask students to begin by tracing a half-circle for the hair and cut it out. Using a handheld mirror, have students observe their hairline, from the forehead to the ears, and sketch it lightly onto the half circle. Then they should cut out the hairline and place the half circle over the face. If the half circle appears too large, they can re-draw the hairline and trim the shape smaller. The final step is to glue down the hair.

Tip: *Show students how to build up longer hair by drawing and cutting out ponytails, braids, and bangs. Encourage them to experiment with cutting, curling, and fringing bangs on the hairline, or with using bows and hair clips to add even more personality.*

 Create the features. The steps here are only a guide for creating the eyes, nose, and mouth; remember that all the portraits should look different! In fact, a good way to guarantee that students will continue to observe and experiment is to take away the glue and budget about 20 minutes of class time just to create and explore with paper shape variations. Tell students that if they don't like what they make, they can always throw it away and start over—it's just paper!

Tips: ❶ *Encourage students to create some variations on eyes and eyebrows and demonstrate how expressions change when eyes look off to the side or straight ahead, how eyebrows can turn up or down, and how the combination of these two features convey surprise, sadness, joy, sneakiness, or anger.*

❷ *Any remaining paper shapes can be stored in a standard-sized envelope with a student's name on it.*

a) Eyes: Ask students to draw two ovals the same size on white paper. (Tracing the finger holes in a pair of scissors can get them started.) They can use a penny or button to trace a circle of black, brown, blue, or green paper for the iris. Students should decide on the direction of the gaze, and glue down following the proportion chart.

b) Nose: The nose is a difficult shape to draw frontally. Students can try to draw one from observation and cut it out. An easy alternative is to create a simple capital "L" shape and trim it until it looks right on the face. Students can also simply draw the L shape in pencil.

c) Mouth: Have students place the mouth halfway between the bottom of the nose and the chin. Then ask them to trace another circle using the paper cup, and cut the circle into two halves. Students will shape the upper and lower lips by trimming the two half circles smaller. Boys may want to use the same skin color as the face, while girls frequently choose red or pink. Encourage experimentation with shape and placement of the lips to explore how lips look smiling, talking, or shouting. A slip of white paper under the lips will create teeth.

d) Eyebrows: This is the easiest and one of the most expressive features to make. Ask students to observe the curve and thickness of the eyebrow and trim to size.

Finish the Project

✳ Invite students to add special touches that bring out personality, such as eyelashes, beauty marks, initials, or a special pendant.

✳ Show students how to add color touches over the construction paper with pencil, marker, or crayon.

Display It!

✺ Paper self-portraits staple easily to bulletin boards. Use double-stick tape to attach them to walls.

✺ Create a "How Are We Feeling Today?" board. Display portraits with synonyms for feelings. Elicit as many words as your class can think of for a mood; have them create sentences using synonyms to show the range of human expression both visually and in the written word.

Art and Language Extensions

✺ Have students tear all the paper shapes instead of cutting them to create "Wild Man" portraits. Torn paper has an energy that cut paper doesn't convey.

✺ Introduce students to the art of Romare Bearden, who used photographs extensively in his collages. Photograph your students, and enlarge the photos digitally or on a copier. Cut out the features from the photographs and integrate them into the project.

✺ Create "10 years from now" portraits so students can project how they might look in the future.

✺ Project a photograph of a student with an overhead projector, and let students trace the enlarged features onto paper. Using the tracing as a guide, they can color and collage on top of it.

✺ Ask students to write descriptions of their appearance as if they had to describe themselves over the phone to a relative they have never met, whom they plan to meet at a train station. Display descriptions as captions to the portraits.

✺ Invite students to write a little vignette that describes a time when they displayed a strong emotion.

Investigate Further

Who created collage? Students can research the history of collage in art, beginning with the breakthroughs of Picasso and Georges Braque. Henri Matisse made innovations in his "Jazz" series. American pop artists, including Warhol and Rauschenberg, continued the use of collage techniques in two-dimensional forms and in "assemblages." Romare Bearden integrated photographed features in his collage portraits. Invite students to create a gallery of collage artists and present their findings.

Book Links

Art Activity Pack: Matisse by Mila Boutan (Chronicle Books, 1996)

Art Activity Pack: Picasso by Mila Boutan (Chronicle Books, 1998)

Collage Techniques, a Guide for Artists and Illustrators by Gerald Brommer (Watson-Guptill Publications, Inc., 1994)

500 Self Portraits edited by Julian Bell (Phaidon Press, 2000) A chronological survey of self-portraits from ancient Egypt to the twentieth century

Looking at Paintings: Self Portraits by Peggy Roalf and Jacques Rowe (Hyperion Books for Children, 1993)

EVALUATE THE PROJECT

1. The student created a collage self-portrait which contains elements that contribute to a recognizable likeness.

    1   2   3   4

2. The student's portrait conveys emotion, a mood, or a sense of personality.

    1   2   3   4

3. The student's use of texture, pattern, color, and overlapping shapes create a visually exciting composition.

    1   2   3   4

EXTENSION EVALUATIONS

1. The student's autobiographical writing and/or descriptions are detailed, accurate, and engaging.

    1   2   3   4

(Scale of 1 to 4; 4 indicates mastery, 1 indicates lack of comprehension or achievement)

How to Create a Self-Portrait

Create an oval for the head.

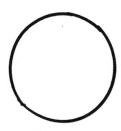

Trace a circle.   Fold.   Cut.   Unfold.

Tuck the neck under the shoulders and glue both of them down.

Glue the head so it sits above the neck and overlaps it.

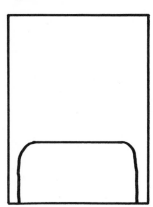
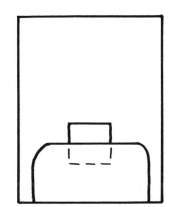

Add the ears.

Add the hair.

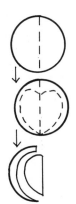

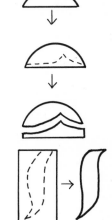

Add the eyes and eyebrows.

Eyes

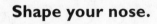

Eyebrows

Shape your nose.

Realistic nose

Abstract nose

L

Shape your mouth.

Mouth

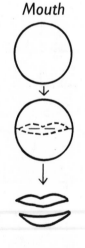

Use both halves or just use the lower lip.

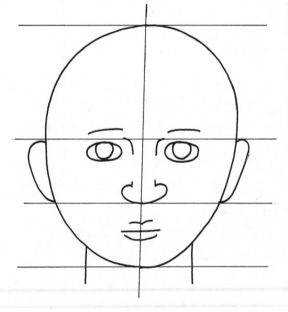

Proportions of the human face

Imagine a line that goes horizontally across the face in the middle. Notice that the top of the eyes and ears are set at this line. The mouth is set halfway between the bottom of the nose and chin. A width of about one eye separates the eyes.

See Yourself in History: Egyptian Self-Portraits

Create a self-portrait in the style of the ancient Egyptians

Middle-school students are into fashion, jewelry, and looking good. The costumes of ancient Egypt are exotic, yet appeal to modern taste. And just as with Egyptian royalty, clothing for adolescents carries the symbolic meaning of social status. Adolescents can explore and try on images of power and sensuality through Egyptian art, bringing learning about an ancient culture into a personal perspective. This idea of "dress up" is adaptable to many other cultures and periods of history as well.

What Students Will Learn and Do

* Draw a picture of themselves as a man or woman living in ancient Egypt.
* Learn about styles of and the symbolic meaning of clothing, jewelry, and head gear from Egyptian culture.
* Learn about the system of gods and goddesses in ancient Egyptian myths.

Materials

Egyptian Profiles coloring/drawing reproducible, page 26

How to Draw an Egyptian Portrait reproducible page 27

Large sheets of drawing paper (24" x 36"), one per student, or long roll of drawing paper

Colored pencils, markers, or crayons

Erasers, rulers, masking tape

Overhead projector or slide projector

Pictures of ancient Egyptian costumes

Vocabulary

self-portrait: a picture that you draw of yourself

profile: the outline of the human head when seen from the side

ancient: belonging to a very early period of history

pharaoh: a ruler of ancient Egypt

hieroglyphics: a system of picture writing used by the ancient Egyptians

amulet: a charm, necklace or bracelet that is adorned with magical symbols and designed to protect the wearer from evil

ankh: a cross having a loop at the top; symbol of eternal life in ancient Egypt

scarab: a kind of beetle whose image was used as a symbol of resurrection in ancient Egypt

Get the Class Thinking

Adventure movies, such as "The Mummy" and "The Scorpion King" have made images of ancient Egypt popular in the adolescent imagination, and you can use photographs or video clips to introduce the topic. Questions such as "What aspects of Egyptian costumes look modern to you?" help to relate ancient fashions to how adolescents dress today. Answers may include taking note of eye shadow, lipstick, necklaces, ankle bracelets, tattoos, beading and braiding of hair, and so forth.

Explain that the class will draw themselves as ancient Egyptians and that portrait paintings in ancient Egypt were always done in profile.

Getting Started

Distribute copies of Egyptian Profiles reproducible. Ask students to draw pictures of Egyptian costumes on $8\frac{1}{2}$" x 11" drawing paper, and study details of Egyptian art.

> **Tip:** *Pictures of Egyptian costumes are available from the Internet, art books, and museum catalogs. You can also find coloring books of Egyptian art and costumes and prepare additional reproducible pages by photocopying a page from the coloring book. Use whiteout to paint out the details inside the profiled contour of the figure and photocopy the page again. Students will then have to study the details in the photographs and draw them rather than merely color in the figures. This experience makes for excellent preparatory drawings for use in the life-size shadow tracings. If you don't have the time or space to make large portraits, these small drawings can be colored in as a finished piece for display.*

Let's Create!

1 **Trace the students' profiles onto the 24" x 36" paper.** Tape the paper to the chalkboard horizontally or vertically. Have a student stand in front of the paper and assume a pose, head turned in profile, while the shoulders face front. The student's arms and hands should emulate any of the characteristic poses of the ancient Egyptians. Turn on the overhead or slide projector to cast the students' shadow onto the paper. Adjust the size of the shadow by moving the projector closer or farther away. The student should stand close to the paper so that the cast shadow is sharp.

Tip: *Since Egyptian clothing contours are smooth and tight fitting, remove any bulky jackets, sweatshirts, or sweaters before beginning. Erase any bumps from the contour that don't look good. Pairs of students can trace each other, freeing you to help other students.*

See Egyptian Profiles (page 26) and How to Draw an Egyptian Portrait (page 27) for visual instructions.

2. **Draw costumes, jewelry, and details onto the large profile tracing.** Students can use their preparatory drawings or photographs for reference.

3. **Draw the face on the portrait.** Follow this sequence:

a) Ears: Have students place the ears in the center of the head turned in profile. The ear generally has the shape of a half-heart rather than a 'C' shape. The top of the ear is level with the eyebrow, the bottom of the ear is level with the nostrils.

b) Hair: Small bumps on the profile can be used to indicate the hairline on the forehead. Students can change their hairline or style if they wish, as Egyptian men and women both wore wigs. Hair can go above or cover the ears.

c) Eyes: The Egyptian eye is represented looking forward, but placed on a profiled head. It is a cat's eye, or almond in shape. Add eye makeup and a full eyebrow. Both men and women wore makeup in ancient Egypt.

d) Nose: The nostrils can be drawn with a curved line. In Egyptian religion the nostrils were considered the entryway of the soul, or "Ka," which was carried on the breath.

e) Lips: Boys can draw their lips with a single line. The girls can draw and color their lips to look as if they are wearing lipstick.

4. **Draw objects to hold in the hands:** Ask students to draw a sword, staff, scepter, basket, ankh, and so forth. The objects students choose will designate their figure as a laborer, artisan, or member of royalty.

5. **Create the background.** Encourage students to add a background that reflects ancient Egyptian civilization. Details in the background should be smaller and can include the Nile River, pyramids, temples, camels, hieroglyphics, servants, soldiers, and so forth. Landscape backgrounds should have a horizon line.

Finish the Project

❋ Have students color the portrait with pencil, crayon, or marker. The project also may be painted.

Display It!

❋ Display the portraits side by side, touching, to create the effect of a mural painted on a temple wall.

Art and Language Extensions

- This project can be used to create portraits from any civilization or historical period. Try "dressing up" in the costumes of any of the following:
  - American colonial period
  - The Renaissance
  - Ancient Rome
  - The roaring twenties
  - Ancient China
- Younger students also enjoy researching and dressing themselves in uniforms of adult professions: nurse, doctor, policewoman, fireman, baseball player, and so forth. The background would indicate the place of business: teacher's classroom, veterinarian's office, courtroom. Students can write essays or short stories about how they see themselves in a future career.
- Trace profiles on a wall and paint with acrylic paint to create a permanent mural to beautify your school.

Investigate Further

- Ask students to do independent research and report on various aspects of ancient Egyptian culture:
  - The mummification process
  - The Rosetta stone
  - Symbolic meanings of scarabs, the ankh, the crown of Upper and Lower Egypt
  - The myths and powers of the Egyptian gods Isis, Osiris, Anubis, and Thoth
  - How papyrus is made

Book Links

Fun with Hieroglyphics by Catherine Roehrig (Viking Press, 1990)

Ancient Egyptian Designs: Coloring Book by Ed Sibbett (Dover Publications, Inc., 1981)

Ancient Egyptian Costume Paper Dolls by Tom Tierney (Dover Publications, Inc., 1997)

Egyptian Designs: 390 Different Designs (Dover Publications, Inc., 1999)

EVALUATE THE PROJECT

1. The student drew his or her self-portrait as an ancient Egyptian, with the head in profile and the body turned frontally.

       1   **2**   **3**   **4**

2. The student added relevant and historically accurate details to the portrait.

       1   **2**   **3**   **4**

3. The student created a background that sets the portrait in the context of ancient Egyptian civilization.

       1   **2**   **3**   **4**

(Scale of 1 to 4; 4 indicates mastery, 1 indicates a lack of comprehension or achievement)

Egyptian Profiles

Add details to complete the figures.

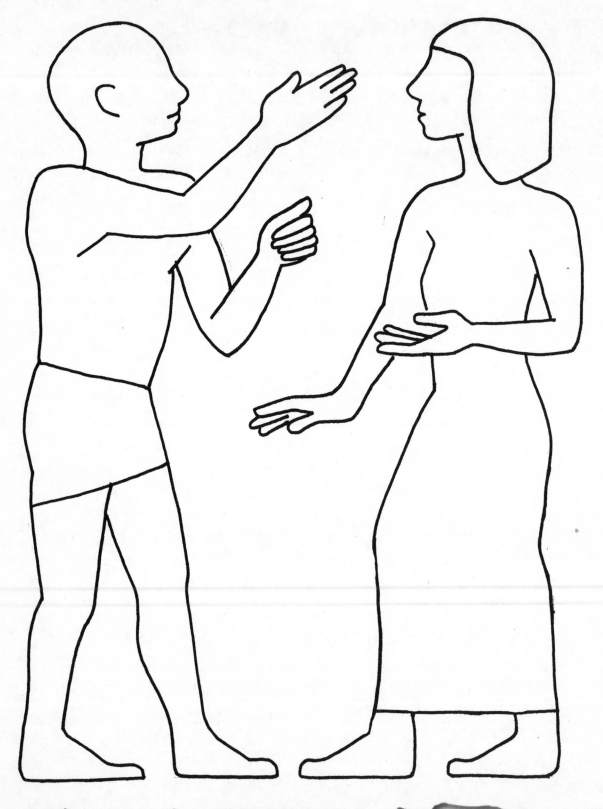

How to Draw an Egyptian Portrait

Pose and trace your profile.

Locate the ear and hairline.

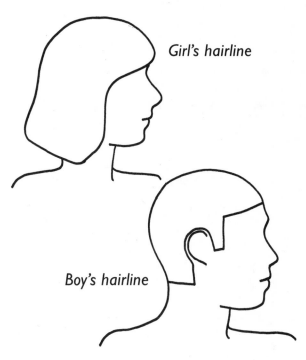

Girl's hairline

Boy's hairline

Draw an ancient Egyptian-style eye.

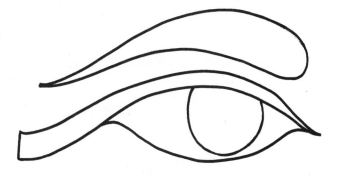

Finish the face by adding a nostril and lips. Add details to the hair such as braiding.

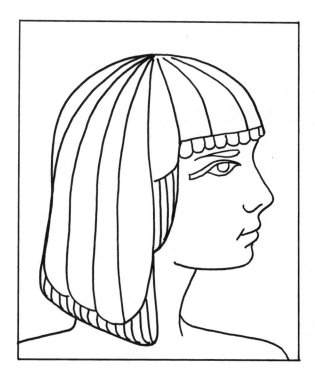

Beauty in Your Name: Designing With Stencils

Create a two-dimensional pattern with alphabet stencils

Students who feel anxious about drawing will often respond to projects that result in beautiful images through a specific format, such as pattern making. Here is a pattern-making project that students personalize by using their names within it.

What Students Will Learn and Do

✸ Create a two-dimensional pattern with stencils.

✸ Learn about symmetrical and asymmetrical patterns.

✸ Create a dynamic play between positive and negative spaces.

✸ Examine artwork that makes use of positive/negative space interplay.

Materials

How to Design With Stencils reproducible, page 32

White drawing paper cut to 15" square, one per student

12" or 18" rulers

Alphabet stencils and stencil shapes, assembled in packets

Pencils, markers, scissors, tape

Extra oaktag, 4" square, for creating decorative shapes

Tip: *Purchasing multiple stencil kits for your class can be expensive. Here's how to make your own:*

1. *Buy only one alphabet stencil set from a hardware or office supply store. For this project, the recommended height of the stencils is 3".*

2. *On oaktag or on a manila folder cut to size ($8\frac{1}{2}$" x $11\frac{3}{4}$") draw six boxes approximately 4" square.*

3. *Trace one copy of the same letter of the alphabet into each of the six boxes. (Repeat with the other 25 letters.)*

4. *Use this as a template to run off copies onto other pre-cut file folders.*

5. *Assemble alphabet packs for each group or table in your class.*
   - *Packs can go into a 10" x 14" mailing envelope for storage.*
   - *Remember to run off extra sheets for high frequency consonants and vowels. (a, e, i, o, u, and c, d, f, g, h, m, n, r, s, t)*

Get the Class Thinking

Students will enjoy designing with stencils because the results look neat and professional. When you show them examples of stencil patterns, students will notice that beautiful patterns can be either symmetrical or asymmetrical. Here are some suggested parameters:

※ Repeat the name more than once to create a complex pattern.

※ Every box in the grid should have a color or design.

※ Limit the number of colors to four.

※ Limit freehand drawing in this project. Instead, have students create stencils for any additional shapes they want to use, such as hearts, lightning, money signs, and so forth.

※ Clarify terms such as positive and negative space. For this project, positive space can be defined as the shape of the letter itself. Have your students color around a sample stenciled letter so that they get an idea of the negative space.

Getting Started

1 **Measure a 3" grid** on a 15" square piece of paper, using pencils and rulers.

Tip: *For younger or special education students, a modification to help them measure would be to mark off every 3 inches of the ruler using red tape.*

See How to Design With Stencils reproducible (page 32) for visual directions.

2 **Pick out the letters of the name** that will be used in the pattern from the alphabet pack. Have students cut off the letter they need from the sheet of six, and return the rest to the pack.

3 **Cut out the stencils,** and have students write their name and class on each one.

> Tips: **1** *Some students, and the special education population in particular, may have difficulty cutting out stencils so that they do not fall apart. Model for these students how to cut out a stencil by creating a jumbo-sized stencil of a letter (about 18") and then demonstrate cutting carefully along the black lines.*
>
> **2** *Note that letters with two pieces require that each piece be cut out independently.*
>
> **3** *Point out that students enter and exit the stencil through the same cut. Tape this entry closed to finish the stencil.*

Let's Create!

1 **Play with the possible arrangements of letters by placing the stencils onto the grid without tracing.** Some long names may have to wrap around in an "L" shape, or be stacked in letter groups, to fit inside the grid. Students may want to create their designs as a puzzle in which their names are hidden by repeating the letters.

2 **Explore new patterns by rotating, inverting, and reversing the letters.** Students can make shadows and three-dimensional effects by shifting the stencil slightly, re-tracing, and then connecting the shapes.

3 **Add decorative symbols** to the name design with shape stencils made from oaktag squares.

Finish the Project

☀ **Ask students to add color to finish.** Limiting the colors students use to four helps to keep the overall design readable. Show the class how coloring the negative space around the letters can create dramatic shapes. Have them consider white as color in relation to a colored positive or negative space. Contrast negative and positive spaces by contrasting a bright color against a dark color.

Display It!

☀ Displayed together on a bulletin board or outside in the hall, this project really brightens up a classroom and gives students a sense of ownership.

Art and Language Extensions

☀ Students can use stencils to design personalized book covers and journal covers.

☀ Two friends can measure a large grid and plan a combined design using both of their names.

☀ Younger students and some special education students may benefit from working with larger stencils (5" or 6" high).

Investigate Further

☀ Stenciling is a folk art craft used throughout the world to decorate fabric, walls, floors, and furniture. Challenge your students to search for examples of stencil art around the world, including prehistoric cave art, the art of the Pennsylvania Dutch, Alaskan stencil art, and art found on African adobe walls.

☀ In his art, M.C. Escher makes use of repeated shapes, positive and negative shape interplay, and geometric tessellations in imaginative and surrealistic compositions. Invite your students to investigate and report on the life of this fascinating artist.

Book Links

Stenciling for the First Time by Rebecca Carter (Sterling Publishing Co., Inc., 2000)

Art from Many Hands, Multi-cultural Art Projects by Jo Miles Schuman (Davis Publications, Inc., 1984)

M. C. Escher Coloring Book: 24 Images to Color (Harry Abrams, Inc., 1995)

Web Link

http://www.worldofescher.com/
World of Escher. A complete web site on the artwork of M.C. Escher

---

EVALUATE THE PROJECT

1. The student completed a stencil project using his or her name.

    1   2   3   4

2. The student measured a 3" grid accurately.

    1   2   3   4

3. The student demonstrated how to use positive and negative space with color contrasts to create a dynamic design.

    1   2   3   4

4. The student created a design, either symmetrical or asymmetrical, in which every box in the grid was utilized and contributes to the overall scheme.

    1   2   3   4

(Scale of 1 to 4; 4 indicates mastery, 1 indicates a lack of comprehension or achievement)

How to Design With Stencils

Cut out stencils.

Arrange the letters.

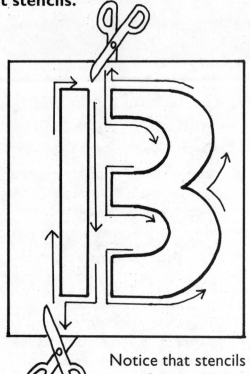

Notice that stencils with two shapes require separate entrances when you cut. Exit through the same cut by which you entered. Then tape the opening closed.

To make shadow letters, shift the stencil, trace again, and then connect the shadow to the original shape.

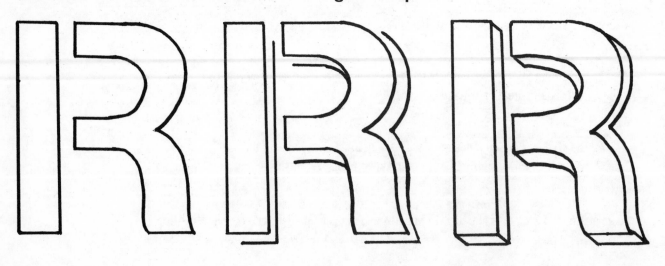

Bigger is Better: Scale Model Butterflies

Create a three-dimensional model of an insect

Butterflies are beautiful in their own small size, but when enlarged, the amazing details of a butterfly's body can be studied and appreciated. This lesson presents opportunities for students to build in scale—approximately five times larger than real life—a detailed model of one of the 15,000 species of butterflies living on this planet.

What Students Will Learn and Do

* Examine drawings of butterflies to learn about the characteristics that define butterflies as insects.
* Learn about the various functions of a butterfly's body parts.
* Learn about the purposes of a butterfly's wing coloration.
* Create a three-dimensional model in scale.
* Develop skills in drawing, painting, and model making.
* Learn how to reverse transfer a pattern.

Materials

Butterfly Wing Patterns reproducible, page 39

How to Create a Model Butterfly reproducible, pages 40–41

Wing Template reproducible, page 42

Color plates or pictures of butterfly species from encyclopedias or other reference sources

Letter size manila folders, one per student

Pipe cleaners, 12" long, brown or black, 5 per student

Newspaper, two sheets per student

Masking tape

Colored pencils, markers, permanent black markers or tempera paint (all colors), and brushes

Charcoal pencils, soft 2B

Proportion wheel (optional)

Tip: *Pictures of butterflies are available in color plates from encyclopedias. Look for color plates that also show the underside of the wing, as the patterns and coloration of the underside are frequently different from the top. Color copy these plates, and slip them inside plastic sleeve protectors. Most color plates will give you a scale to compare the illustrations to life size.*

Get the Class Thinking

If possible, introduce the lesson by having the class examine a real butterfly under a magnifying glass. Ask students what they already know about butterflies. Can they identify the parts of a butterfly's body? Do they know why a butterfly is classified as an insect, along with ants?

Using either a diagram projected on an overhead or a model butterfly you've created, take the class on a tour of the butterfly's anatomy. Have students notice that the underside of the wings is frequently less colorful than the top of the wings. This coloration acts as a natural camouflage when the butterfly folds its wings to rest on a flower to feed.

Unroll the proboscis on the model so students have a sense of its length. Point out that the organs of taste are located on the front legs, while the butterfly smells with its antennae.

Getting Started

Practice drawing butterfly wing patterns. Distribute copies of butterfly color plates or pictures, the Butterfly Wing Patterns reproducible, and color pencils. Students will match the blank wing shape on the reproducible to the color plate/picture. Encourage students to share color plates/pictures and try drawing and coloring the patterns of two or three different species. Make sure that they understand that the color illustrations show the top and the underside of the same wing.

Tip: *It's very helpful to post an illustration pointing out which side represents the top and which side represents the underside. Students will need to use this understanding to create an accurate model.*

Let's Create!

1 **Create the body.** Distribute newspaper and tape. Have students tightly roll up two sheets of newspaper on the short side (to make a 12-inch tube) and tape. There should be no space or light visible within the rolled newspaper tube.

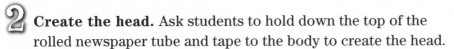

Distribute and refer to How to Create a Model Butterfly (pages 40–41) for visual instructions.

2 **Create the head.** Ask students to hold down the top of the rolled newspaper tube and tape to the body to create the head.

3 **Create the thorax.** Give each student two half sheets of newspaper, folded in half. Have them tape the newspaper sheets to the body under the head and wrap the newspaper around the body. As it becomes thicker, it becomes the thorax. Make sure students tape the sheet closed so that it does not unravel.

4 **Create details of the head: antennae, eyes, and proboscis.** Instruct students to follow this sequence and refer to the steps illustrated on the reproducible how-to pages.

   a) Eyes: Roll two balls of masking tape for the compound eye. Keep the eyes the same size. Tape eyes to either side of the head.

   b) Antennae: Cut a 12" long pipe cleaner in half, curl the top into a knob, fold the bottom into a "L" shape, and tape the two antennae to the top of the head.

   c) Proboscis: Cut a 12" long pipe cleaner in half, curl up one of the halves into a tight spiral, and tape it to the underside of the head.

Tip: *Finishing the head makes a natural end point for the day's activity. Students can write their names on the bodies. Collect and store together in a large bag.*

5 **Create the wings.** Prepare in advance wing templates for students to trace by enlarging copies of each wing type. Four sample common wing shapes are included on the reproducible on page 42. A scale is provided inside each wing shape. Each wing shape will enlarge to fill an $8\frac{1}{2}$" x 11" piece of paper when it is enlarged 200%. Cut out the paper enlargement and use it as a template to trace on a manila folder, aligning the flat edge of the wing with the folded edge of the folder. Then cut out the wing shape on the manila folder. You now have a durable template to slip over other manila folders to trace. With four students to assist you, they can trace about ten of each wing shape, enough for the entire class.

Tip: *An alternate method of enlargement is to use a proportion wheel, available at photography, art, and graphic design stores for about $5.00. This consists of two wheels that rotate one on top of the other. By lining up the size of the original image with the size of the intended enlargement, the percentage of enlargement will appear in the window. Then the percentage can be entered into the copier or scanner you are using.*

6 **Have students pick out the wing that most closely matches the one they practiced drawing.** They should then cut out the wing shape, keeping the folder closed. When they open the folder, ask them to label one side "top of wing," turn it over, and label the other side "underside of wing."

> Tip: *For a stronger wing, repeat step 6 and glue the two wing shapes together to create a double-ply wing. When you apply paint, the double-ply wings will not curl.*

7 **Carefully draw the top wing pattern onto the manila folder.** Students should refer back to the original color illustrations and draw the top wing pattern on the "top of wing" side of their folder.

8 **Transfer the pattern.** After drawing the pattern with pencil, ask students to trace all the lines with a soft 2B charcoal pencil, pressing hard. Then have them close the folder and press and rub the closed folder with their fingertips. When they open the folder, the charcoal lines should have transferred to the other side and the pattern is reversed. Repeat as necessary. Since charcoal lines will be faint, students may need to reinforce them by tracing over the lines with a regular pencil.

> Tip: *Do not use charcoal sticks, which are messier and break easily. Charcoal pencils can be sharpened in a pencil sharpener.*

9 **Label the colors** of the wing in preparation for painting or coloring.

10 **Draw the underside of the wing,** using the color reference illustrations to draw the pattern of the underside of the wing, and then repeat steps 8 and 9.

11 **Tape the wings to the underside of the body** as shown on the how-to reproducible.

12 **Tape the legs to the underside of the body.** Cut 12" pipe cleaners in half, have students bend them into shape, and tape them onto the body as shown on the how-to reproducible.

Finish the Project

When the models are assembled, students can color them. (Again, students should refer back to the original butterfly color plates/pictures.) Options for coloring include magic markers and tempera paint. Colored pencils can be used to add tints over light colors.

- ✹ **Markers:** Students can successfully cover newspaper and masking tape with permanent black magic markers. Regular markers color well over manila folders. Begin with light colors first.

- ✹ **Tempera paint:** Tempera will cover opaquely all the materials used in this project. Have students paint one side of the project at a time, and allow to dry before turning over.

- ✹ **Correction fluid:** Students can use white or colored correction fluid to make small dots and dashes in patterns.

Display It!

The most effective way to display the butterflies created by the class is in flight. Suspend them from lights or overhead pipes using fishing wire or yarn. Find the balance point of the model by balancing it on your finger until it is level, then fold up the wings. Punch out two holes in the wings above the balance point, as shown on the how-to reproducible. Tie the wire or yarn to these holes and suspend the model.

Art and Language Extensions

✸ Have students create other large scale insects, such as ladybugs, ants, dragonflies.

✸ Ask the class to investigate other materials for creating models, including clay, styrofoam, or papier-mâché. They might also try waxed paper wrapped around a wire armature to create translucent wings.

✸ Encourage students to create fantasy insects. Leaving realism behind, students will create a new species of insect. Anything goes, as long as they retain the scientific classification of an insect: an exoskeleton body in three parts, six legs, and wings!

✸ What does the head of a fly look like up close? Invite students to investigate other small living creatures, observe them through a magnifying glass or microscope, and draw them.

Investigate Further

✸ Students can research the natural habitat of the species of the butterfly they have modeled. Questions to research include: Is the species common or rare? Is it migratory? How long is its adult life span? Does it have natural predators? Does it use camouflage? Display their reports alongside the butterfly models.

✸ Ask students to calculate how they would look if they were enlarged 5 times. Create a paper person or mark off dimensions in the hallway to show the sense of scale next to the butterfly models. Calculate how much food such a giant might consume in one day.

Book Links

The Life Cycle of Butterflies: Teacher's Guide by Lynn Miller and Marilyn Fenichel, eds. (National Science Resources Center, Smithsonian Institution, 1992)

Caterpillar Grow Kits: Carolina Biological Supply Company, 2700 York Road, Burlington, NC. 27215 Call 1-800-334-5551

National Audubon Society First Field Guide: Insects Christine Wilsdon, ed. (Scholastic Press, 1998)

Flies Taste with Their Feet: Weird Facts about Insects Melvin Berger, editor (Scholastic Press, 1997)

Dirt and Grime, Like You've Never Seen by Vicki Cobb (Scholastic Press, 1998) Magnifications of dust, mold, mites, and microscopic life.

Web Links

http://www.insects.org/entophiles
Bug Bios web site. Profiles of bugs and insects with photo enlargement capabilities.

http://www.denniskunkel.com
Dennis Kunkel's Microscopy, Inc., web site. An educational resource of stock photography and scientific photography through the microscope

✸ Schedule a visit to a butterfly conservatory: many zoos now feature an enclosed park where you can walk through a tropical environment where butterflies are flying freely.

✸ Raise caterpillars into butterflies, observing the life cycle. See Book and Web Links (page 37) for ordering information.

EVALUATE THE PROJECT

1. The student created a scale model of a butterfly approximately 5 times greater than life size.

    1   2   3   4

2. The student carefully observed the details, patterns, and colors of the species. Student's model and drawings can be identified as a particular species.

    1   2   3   4

3. The student can identify the anatomical features of an insect.

    1   2   3   4

(Scale of 1 to 4; 4 indicates mastery, 1 indicates lack of comprehension or achievement)

Butterfly Wing Patterns

Match the shape of the butterfly's wing pattern in your color picture to one of the wing patterns below. Practice drawing your butterfly's pattern inside.

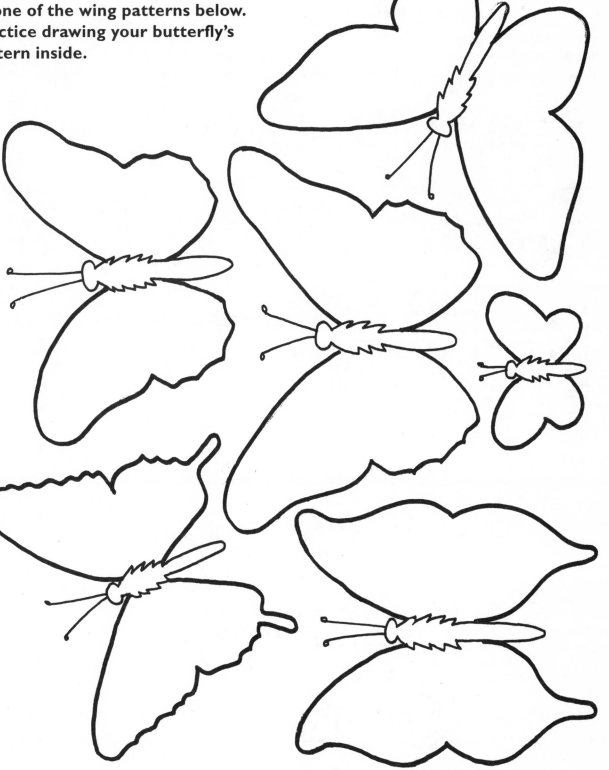

How to Create a Model Butterfly

Draw the wing patterns.

Note: the top side and the underside of butterflies' wings are frequently very different. Label the side you draw as either "top" or "underside."

Underside   *Top*

Create the body by rolling, folding, and taping newspaper.

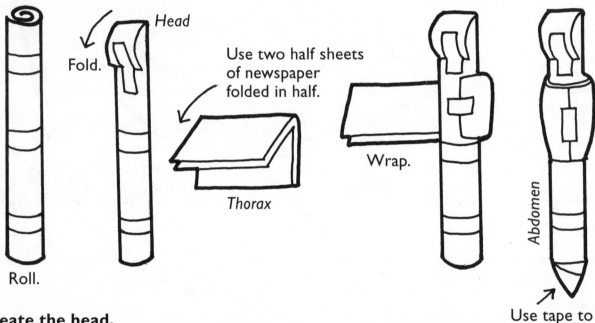

Roll.

Fold.   *Head*

Use two half sheets of newspaper folded in half.

Thorax

Wrap.

Abdomen

Use tape to make a point.

Create the head.

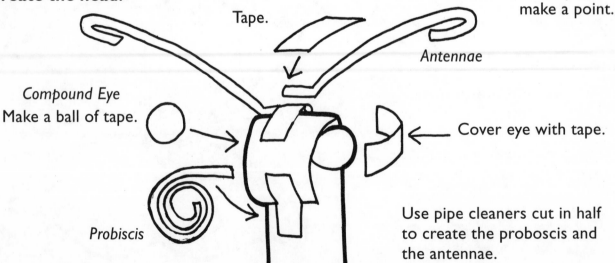

Tape.

Antennae

Compound Eye
Make a ball of tape.

Cover eye with tape.

Probiscis

Use pipe cleaners cut in half to create the proboscis and the antennae.

40

Transfer the wing pattern.

Draw the
wing pattern.

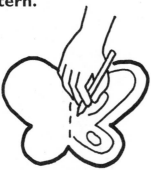

Trace over with a
charcoal pencil.

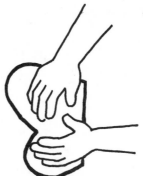

Fold, press, and
rub to transfer.

Copy faint lines
with a pencil.

Tape the wings to the body.

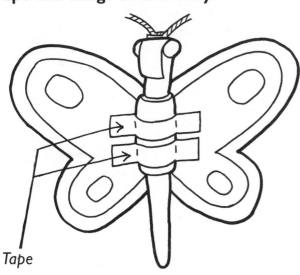

Tape

Tape the legs to the body.

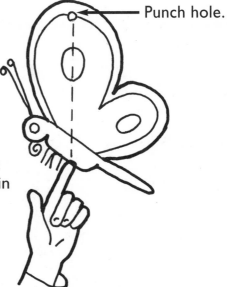

Punch hole.

To finish and display: Find the
balance point. Punch a hole in each
wing, tie two ends of a long string in
the holes, and hang the butterfly.

Wing Template

Monarch or Milkweed
(North America)

(On 8 $\frac{1}{2}$" folder:
enlarge 200%,
5 times natural size.)

Tiger Swallowtail
(North America)

(On 8 $\frac{1}{2}$" folder:
enlarge 200%,
5 times natural size.)

Common Sulphur
(North America)

(On 8 $\frac{1}{2}$" folder:
enlarge 200%,
5 times natural size.)

Morpho Rhetenor
(Central America)

(On 8 $\frac{1}{2}$" folder:
enlarge 200%,
5 times natural size.)

Thirsty?
Design a Soda Can!

Create an original soda can label following design and measurement parameters

Design is everywhere: in the clothing we wear, the items we purchase, the cars we drive, and the chairs we sit on. As they design an original can label in this project, students receive a simple introduction to the world of design and begin to consider the concept of design parameters. Since your students probably like soda (soft drinks), it's easy to motivate them to do this project—and it's an easy one to create, too.

What Students Will Learn and Do

* Create an original soda can label.
* Follow design and measurement parameters.
* Use graphic design elements—lettering, layout, and color—to present a product.
* Work with brand names, an image, and a slogan to create a market identity.
* Write a catchy slogan.
* Learn about nutritional listing requirements in foods.

Materials

Setting Parameters & Making Plans (Soda Can Label) reproducible, page 48

How to Create Your Soda Can Label reproducible, page 49

Empty soda cans, one for each student, rinsed clean and dry

STANDARDS

Visual Arts

Standard 4: Understands the visual arts in relation to history and cultures.

English Language Arts

Standard 4: Adjusts use of spoken, written, and visual language to communicate effectively with a variety of audiences.

White paper for labels, precut to $8\frac{1}{2}$" × $3\frac{3}{4}$"
(three labels can be cut from one sheet of paper)
Scotch tape, colored pencils, markers, fine-tip
permanent markers

Get the Class Thinking

Poll students about which sodas they like best. Play a guessing game to introduce visual design: present cans of soda with the brand name covered by tape. Most students will still be able to identify the brand of soda instantly. Ask them to name the other ways we recognize a product, besides by the name. For example, specific colors are identified with certain brands: Coke is a specific red, 7UP is green, while Pepsi is always blue. Logos and pictures also identify the brand. Some logos, such as the Nike "swoosh," are so famous that the brand name doesn't have to be seen.

Form design parameters: Discussing with students what makes a good soda can label can help them uncover the design parameters that make the design work. Distribute and refer to the parameters provided on the Setting Parameters and Making Plans reproducible (page 48) to guide the discussion. The class may agree that a good label has the following:

- ❋ a good name for an original flavor
- ❋ a readable font (lettering)
- ❋ colors and pictures incorporated into the design
- ❋ a fun and exciting feeling
- ❋ a catchy slogan
- ❋ a list of ingredients and a nutrition label

Encourage students to examine these criteria, evaluate an actual soda can, and get specific. Should the name be completely original? Can the soda be a combination of two flavors to make an original flavor? From how far away should you be able to read the name? What limit on colors would you place?

Tip: *Students can answer many of these questions for themselves by examining the cans. For example, they may notice that soda cans are printed in two or three colors plus black and white.*

You may choose not to use the parameter reproducible and allow the class to create their own design parameters to follow by charting the results of this class discussion.

Vocabulary

design (verb): to plan how something will look and work

design (noun): an arrangement of elements, such as shapes and colors, in a product or work of art; a plan

graphic design: the arrangement of pictures and text upon a page or label

parameters: the guidelines, or limits, you must follow to create a design project

logo: a symbol for a company

slogan: a short sentence or phrase that helps you to remember a product

color contrast: light objects placed on a dark background or dark objects placed on a light background

Getting Started

1 **Check that students understand the design parameters before beginning the project.**

2 **It's writing time!** Distribute the reproducible planning page (page 48). Allow students time to brainstorm several ideas for a product. Encourage them to create unusual combinations of flavors and names. Tell them that they can always change their minds as new ideas come to them.

Distribute How to Create Your Soda Can Label (page 49) for visual instructions.

Let's Create!

1 **Select one product idea and sketch design ideas on the precut white paper.** Ask students to box off a rectangular section at one end (about 2" wide) and reserve this box for the nutrition facts and ingredients.

> **Tip:** *It's a good idea to have students first work at spacing and lettering their product name. The letters will have to be big so that they are readable from at least 10 feet away, but the entire name also has to be visible on the side of the can facing you. Have students examine the cans to see how names are placed diagonally or vertically. Students may have to rework their ideas a few times to get the name to fit, so encourage them to make a number of rough sketches before they decide on a final design.*

2 **Wrap the label around an empty soda can to see how it looks.** Have students repeat as necessary.

> **Tip:** *It's not necessary to give out 25 empty cans. One can per group of four students will do. And for those students who can't stop banging, dropping, or crushing those cans, keep their empty cans in the front of the class. Wrap the labels for the students and hold up the can for them to evaluate.*

3 **Add a drawing, shapes, or pictures to the label and create a slogan.** Remind the class that the drawing and slogan should relate to the name and flavor of the soda.

4 **Add color.** Colored pencil shapes outlined with magic marker work well for this project.

> **Tip:** *Show students how to keep the label readable by giving a mini-lesson on color contrasts. Note that soda cans like Diet Coke, which have the brand name in a dark color, have a light colored or silver background. Cans with brand names in white, such as Classic Coke, have a dark background. Discourage dark on dark color combinations, unless each area is separated and outlined by a thick white line. Light on light combinations can be highlighted with a dark outline.*

5 **Add the nutrition facts and ingredients inside the box.** Make sure students check their spelling!

Finish the Project

* Have students use scotch tape to anchor their labels to an empty soda can. After they secure one end to the can, have them wrap the label around and tape the second end to the label.

* Write the students' names on the bottom of the cans with a permanent magic marker.

Display It!

* Finished cans look great set up side by side or stacked.

* Create a store-front display with student writing and grocery store style "big bursts" displayed next to the cans.

Art and Language Extensions

* Ask students to write a short commercial for their soda or set their soda slogan to music. Have them evaluate 30-second commercials for popular sodas and use these as models.

* Challenge the class by having the project presented as a design contest: prizes or certificates could be awarded for the most original name, most unusual flavor, best overall design, or funniest presentation. Take a class vote for the contest winners.

* Keep designing! Now that students have an idea of how to design within parameters, what else could they do? Challenge students to draw designs for any of the following:

  * Belts and belt buckles (Challenge them to find new ways to hold pants up!)
  * Currency (How would they design their own image of wealth?)
  * A boom box, CD player, or a remote control. (Where would they put all those buttons and controls?)
  * Hats (How can they provide protection from the sun or cold?)
  * Sneakers (What's the next cool look?)

* Try out the recipe! Students may ask you if they can make their own sodas with the ingredients they listed. My own students were fascinated by trying one another's concoctions. Some of my students' flavor combinations have turned out pretty bizarre, but surprisingly tasty. All you need is a blender, seltzer, sugar, a spoon, and some paper cups. Have students bring in their flavorings and set aside the last 15 minutes of the class for this fun activity. It will be one wrap-up activity they won't forget!

Investigate Further

☼ Have students research the meaning of several words in the nutrition facts panel. For example:

- Why are **proteins** and **carbohydrates** necessary for the body?
- How many milligrams of **sodium** should a person have on a daily basis if one can of soda provides 2% of the minimum daily requirement?
- How do you **carbonate** water?
- How do artificial sweeteners work? Which have been found safe for consumption?

Students might call the consumer information number provided on the can as part of their research.

Book Links

The Total Package: The Secret History and Hidden Meanings of Boxes, Bottles, Cans and Other Persuasive Containers by Thomas Hine and Michael Pietsch (Little, Brown & Co., 1997)

Fifty Trade Secrets of Great Design Packaging by Stafford Cliff (Rockport Publishers, Inc., 1999)

Web Link

http://www.gono.com/vir-mus/museum.htm
The Museum of Beverage Containers and Advertising, Nashville, Tennessee

EVALUATE THE PROJECT

1. The student completed a soda can label with an original name and flavor.

    1   2   3   4

2. The student's brand name is readable from at least ten feet away and fits on the can.

    1   2   3   4

3. The student's overall design, name, brand color, and image work together to create a marketable identity.

    1   2   3   4

EXTENSION EVALUATIONS

1. The student wrote a commercial or a short musical jingle for their slogan.

    1   2   3   4

(Scale of 1 to 4; 4 indicates mastery, 1 indicates lack of comprehension or achievement)

Setting Parameters & Making Plans

(Soda Can Label)

PARAMETERS

These are the design guidelines to help you create your original product.

- ✔ The flavor of the soda must be original. It can be a combination of two flavors.

- ✔ The name of the soda must be original.

- ✔ The name, color, drawings, and design of the label should relate to the flavor of the soda.

- ✔ You must be able to see the entire brand name of the soda on the side of the can.

- ✔ You must be able to read the brand name from ten feet away.

- ✔ You are limited to using three colors plus black and white.

- ✔ You must include the nutrition facts, ingredients, and fluid ounces on the label.

- ✔ The slogan for your soda should appear on the can.

PLANNING QUESTIONS

These questions will help you plan an eye-catching soda can design. Write your answers in a journal or on loose-leaf paper.

1. What flavor, or combination of flavors, will your soda be? (List six ideas.)

2. What will the name of your soda be? Think about the flavor of your soda, and/or the feeling you want associated with your soda. (List six ideas.)

3. What will you draw on your label for your soda? Think again about the flavor, and/or the feeling associated with the soda. (List six ideas.)

4. What ingredients will your soda have?

5. What will be the slogan for your soda? (Remember to keep the slogan short. If your slogan is funny, even better! Think of three ideas.)

How to Create Your Soda Can Label

Sample Layouts

(These examples appear smaller than the actual label size.)

Paper label dimensions: $8\frac{1}{2}$" x $3\frac{3}{4}$"

The visible area of label is approximately $2\frac{1}{2}$" wide.

Nutrition Facts:
Calories 140
Fluid Oz 12

Carbonated Water, Sugar, Strawberry and cranberry

BLAST BERRY

A flavor explosion

| Nutrition facts | Name brand | Slogan | Picture |

Allow for a $\frac{1}{4}$" overlap on the label when taping.

Pick it up never put it down

JAZZ JAZZ

calories 100
Fluid Oz: 12
Ingredients:
carbonated water, sugar, rasberry juice, citric acid

"Gotta Have My Tunes": Design an Original CD Cover

Create an original CD cover with liner notes

Middle school students are passionate about music. If you've ever overheard students argue the merits of one performer over another, or asked them to put away the headphones in class, then you know you can motivate them on this music-based project.

Designing an original CD cover can expose students to related careers in graphic design, photography, illustration, copy writing, song writing, sound production, and art direction.

What Students Will Learn and Do

- ☀ Create an original CD cover with liner notes.
- ☀ Organize pictures, title, colors, and text to create a mood or fit a theme.
- ☀ Learn about the concepts of graphic design and layout.
- ☀ Write original song titles.
- ☀ Write sample verses for an original song.

STANDARDS

Visual Arts

Standard 1: Understands and applies media, techniques, and processes related to the visual arts.

Standard 5: Understands the characteristics and merits of one's own artwork and the artwork of others.

Mathematics

Measurement: Applies appropriate techniques, tools, and formulas to determine measurements.

English Language Arts

Standard 5: Employs a wide range of strategies as he/she writes and uses different writing process elements.

Standard 12: Uses spoken, written, and visual language to accomplish his/her own purposes.

Materials

Setting Parameters & Making Plans (CD cover) reproducible, page 55

How to Create Your CD Cover reproducible, page 56

Pictures from magazines or downloaded from the Internet

Glue sticks, masking tape, pencils, pens, fine line permanent markers, colored pencils

Rulers ($\frac{1}{4}$" scale)

Practice paper (white copier paper will do) cut to $9\frac{3}{4}$" x $4\frac{3}{4}$"

White poster board for finished CD cover, one per student, cut to $9\frac{3}{4}$" x $4\frac{3}{4}$"

Extra posterboard to create viewfinders, cut to same dimensions (optional)

> **Tip:** *Ask each student to bring in an empty CD jewel case to frame a CD cover. If you choose to purchase CD cases yourself, packs of 25, 50, and 100 are available at computer supply stores.*

Vocabulary

graphic design: the arrangement of pictures and text upon a page

layout or **mechanical:** a piece of finished artwork and text ready for reproduction

title track: the song whose title is also the title of the album

theme: the message and feeling of the CD, created by a combination of the music, lyrics, pictures, and colors

Get the Class Thinking

Kick off a discussion about music with these questions: How many different kinds of music can you think of? (Responses may include rap, hip-hop, house, Latin, jazz, world, rock, metal, alternative rock, folk, classical, country, and blues.) What performers do you listen to and care about? Why is this particular performer or group a favorite? What is it about their message, or the feeling that your favorite songs convey, that makes you pay attention?

Show samples of CD covers and ask students how photography, illustration, color, and title combine to create a mood. How is the mood continued inside the CD booklet? Emphasize that the look of an album can influence sales as much as the performer or the music itself.

Explain to students that they will design an original CD for their favorite performer or group. The idea is to come up with a new idea for the next album from that performer or group, including 10 to 12 original song titles.

Getting Started

Distribute the Setting Parameters and Making Plans reproducible. Go over the suggested parameters with students, allow them time to consider the questions, and have them write a list of 10 to 12 possible song titles.

> **Tips:** ❶ *Students should be aware of the style of music and themes of the performer or group that they picked. Encourage them to use elements of that style to generate song titles that are plausible for that group.*
>
> ❷ *Sometimes students will want to make dance party compilations, pair two performers together, or cast themselves as the performer in a debut CD. Allow*

students to pursue these ideas, provided that they have a firm idea of the musical style and themes they will use.

3 *Remind students to avoid song lyrics and images that promote violence, drug use, bigotry, or abuse.*

Distribute and refer to How to Create Your CD Cover reproducible (page 56) for visual instructions.

Let's Create!

1 **Guide students to select images for their CD covers.** Gather photos of favorite performers from various sources:

* Students can bring in magazines or download pictures from fan sites on the Internet. Allow students to begin their research a week or two before beginning this project.

* You can provide some magazines. Look for free magazines and posters available at big chain music and record stores.

* Students select the image of the performer or group they've chosen for their CD cover. They may either use the image as a model to draw from and skip step 2 or work directly with the image as a collage element (step 2).

2 **(Optional) Create a viewfinder and select photos.** Cut a 4" square window in the center of the posterboard. Show students how to place their viewfinder over the pictures to help them decide how to crop and edit. When they've found the view they like, have them cut out the image accordingly.

Tip: *Photos can be stored in a mailing envelope.*

3 **Design the cover.** Fold over the pre-cut practice paper into a booklet. Let students arrange the photograph (or drawing), album title, performer's or group's name, and artwork. All their planning should be done in pencil only, to permit revisions. They can hold the photo or drawing in place with a small loop of masking tape on its back. The How to Create Your CD Cover reproducible offers several layout ideas.

4 **Design the back.** On the back of the practice paper, ask students to arrange the list of song titles and to integrate artwork.

Tip: *Have lots of pre-cut practice paper ready, as students will go through multiple ideas on practice paper. It helps to have published CD covers and booklets available so they can see many different ways text and images can be combined.*

5 **Design the inside.** Have students consider how to continue the mood with images and colors inside their CD cover. Ask them to include liner notes crediting musicians, the producer, the engineer, and the recording studio, as well as lyrics to one song or just a lyric sample. Be sure they don't forget to list acknowledgments and thank yous, too.

Tip: *Some of this information, such as the names of the contributors and the recording studio, can be taken from a previous CD by the same performer. You can also encourage students to make up as much of the information as they like, such as the recording date.*

Finish the Project

6 **Fold the pre-cut white posterboard into a booklet, with the glossy side serving as the cover and the flat side facing in.** Have students check which side is glossy and which is flat.

7 **Rule $\frac{1}{4}$" guide lines on the back and inside to make "write on" lines for the text.** Show students how to place the $\frac{1}{4}$" scale ruler along the left and right side, mark every quarter inch, and connect the marks horizontally.

8 **Design the finished cover.** Glue down the magazine photo onto the glossy cover using a glue stick. Encourage students to copy their writing and illustrations in pencil first. The album title and performer's name can also be computer generated and then glued down.

Tips: **1** *When students add color, remind them to use light colors behind text.*

2 *Fine line markers and pens will add definition and contrast to their artwork.*

3 *Photographs can be changed by adding color, or drawing directly on top of the surface.*

4 *Magic markers on glossy paper will take about ten seconds to dry—be careful not to smudge. Permanent markers work best.*

9 **Design the back and the inside.** Follow tips for step 3.

Tip: *Students should continue to check for legibility and spelling at this stage.*

Display It!

Slip the finished CD cover in the jewel case for display. Students will love arranging the CDs on a shelf as if they were in a music store.

Art and Language Extensions

✺ Invite students to develop their initial writing about their favorite performers into polished persuasive essays.

✺ Ask students to develop the lyric sample inside the CD into a complete song. Show students how the traditional parts a popular song (verse, refrain, bridge) work together.

✺ Have students write an advertisement for this new CD to promote it. Use fliers from music stores and catalog services as models for product description, style, artwork, and layout.

Book Links

Magazines include: *Seventeen, Teen, Teen People, Vibe, XXL, Tiger Beat, Black Beat, Rolling Stone, Pulse* (Please preview for appropriateness.)

Web Links

http://www.cdcovers.cc/covers.php
Thousands of CD covers and artwork on file

To find biographical information about specific performers and groups, enter their name as a keyword into a search engine.

Investigate Further

☀ Have students research the life of their favorite performer or group through magazine and web sites and compose a biography and recording history.

☀ Encourage students to research and present biographical reports of ground-breaking figures in music: Hank Williams, B. B. King, Lead Belly, Elvis Presley, The Beatles, and so on.

EVALUATE THE PROJECT

1. The student completed a CD cover, with an original album title and 10 to 12 original song titles.

    1   **2**   **3**   **4**

2. The student integrated text, photographs, drawing, color, and layout to create and sustain a mood.

    1   **2**   **3**   **4**

3. The student's song lyrics developed a mood sustained by details and vivid imagery.

    1   **2**   **3**   **4**

EXTENSION EVALUATIONS

1. The student's essay or research was developed into a persuasive essay with interesting details that amplified a main idea.

    1   **2**   **3**   **4**

(Scale of 1 to 4; 4 indicates mastery, 1 indicates a lack of comprehension or achievement)

Setting Parameters & Making Plans

(CD Cover)

PARAMETERS

These are the design guidelines to help you create the CD cover for the next album by your favorite performer or group.

✔ Pick any performer or group that you like.

✔ Think of original titles for the album and 10 to 12 songs. Consider the style and message of your favorite performer or group so that the titles you choose are believable.

✔ Create song titles and images that are free from profanity and abusive language and that don't promote violence or drug use.

✔ Include the following on the outside of the CD booklet:

 1. Photograph or drawing of the performer or group

 2. Title of the album

 3. Name of the performer or group

 4. Song list on back

✔ Include the following on the inside of the CD cover:

 1. A quote or lyric sample from the title track.

 2. Credits to the performers and songwriters: Who is responsible for each song on the album?

 3. Liner notes that credit the producer, sound engineer, and the recording studio.

 4. Acknowledgments: a list of people whom your performer(s) might want to thank.

✔ Write your CD copy neatly by hand or on a word-processing program.

PLANNING QUESTIONS

These questions will help you plan your original cover design. Write your answers in a journal or on loose-leaf paper.

1. Think about your favorite performer or group. Why is this person or group your favorite? Why is this music important to you? What feelings do you get from listening to their music?

2. Most performers have a message in their music that they want to convey. Some messages are simple ("Let's have fun"); some are about the problems of growing up; some are angry; some are political ("Let's change this"). What do you think is the message that your favorite performer(s) wants to express?

3. Think of a theme that will unify all the songs in your new album. What will be your theme?

4. In your journal list 10 to 12 working titles for this album. You can always change your mind later. Which title would you select as the title track? What will be the name of your album?

How to Create Your CD Cover

Create a viewfinder. Use it to find a great angle or view and crop the picture you've chosen.

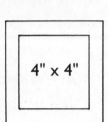

4" x 4"

BLU CITY

NORA JONES

1 ANOTHER MORNING
2 BLU CITY
3 NO PLACE TO HIDE
4 STEPPIN' ON THE CRACKS
5 OVER EASY
6 NOTHIN' THE MATTER
7 YOUR FAVORITE PLACE
8 I GOTTA KNOW NOW
9 AUTUMN IN THE BRONX
10 TELL ME SOMETHING
11 IT WILL BE BETTER
12 IN RESTFUL PLACES

Plan a sample layout.

Front

❋ title of album

❋ photograph or drawing of the performer or group

❋ name of the performer or group

Back

❋ Song List

Inside

❋ Sample verses from the title track

❋ Acknowledgments

❋ Song credits

❋ Credits to musicians

❋ Producer's name and recording information

OUTSIDE MY WINDOW
A BLUE LIGHT SHINES
SHINES ON THIS COLD, WET STREET
SHINES ON THE PEOPLE I MEET
SHINES ON THE BED I SLEEP
AND ILLUMINATES MY MIND

IT'S A BLUE CITY, I KNOW
IT'S A BLUE WORLD, I CRY
IT'S A BLUE FACE I GREET
IN THE MIRROR OF MY MIND

THANKS TO MY MOM, DAD,
PRODUCER EDDIE AND THE LORD!

ALL SONGS WRITTEN BY
NORA JONES

VOCALS — NORA JONES
ACOUSTIC BASS — LONNIE PLAXICO
ALTO SAXOPHONE — STEVE COLEMAN
PERCUSSION — MINO CINELU
ELECTRIC GUITAR — MARVIN SEWELL
DRUMS — MARCUS BAYLOR

PRODUCED BY ED GERRARD
RECORDED AT THE HIT FACTORY
OCTOBER 2005

It's Amazing! Paper Mazes

Design and construct a paper maze

If your students like to trick you or stump each other with puzzles, then they'll love to build their own mazes and test them. This simple project offers a good introduction to three-dimensional design and challenges students to consider the interplay between positive and negative spaces found in architectural design.

What Students Will Learn and Do

* Design and construct a paper maze.
* Measure and draw a 1" square grid.
* Cut and position accurately.
* Learn about the concepts of positive and negative space, solid and void.
* Research the history, uses, and cultural significance of mazes and labyrinths.

Materials

Maze Planning Sheet reproducible, page 61
How to Construct Your Maze reproducible, page 62
Manila folders, pre-cut to 8" x 11", one per student
Colored index cards, 3" x 5", 20 cards per student
Glue, scissors, scotch tape, rulers, pencils
Small balls or marbles
Timer

Get the Class Thinking

The best way to motivate the class is to try to trick them with a maze that you've created. Have volunteers come up, drop a small ball or marble into the entrance of the maze, and start a timer. How long does it take students to solve your maze? Challenge students to create a trickier, more devious maze than yours.

Ask the class what makes a good maze and see if they can develop their own parameters. (One parameter that is important is that the maze should have only one solution, although it will have many dead ends.)

Find out if students know the difference between a labyrinth and a maze; many people confuse the two.

Pass out copies of the Maze Planning Sheet reproducible on page 61 and let students begin to design their mazes. Demonstrate how to connect the dots on the grid to create the perimeter, openings, barriers, and pathways.

Vocabulary

labyrinth: a single passage that twists and turns on itself in moving toward the center

maze: a confusing network of passages with many dead ends

grid: a network of evenly spaced horizontal and perpendicular lines

positive space: space that is filled with a solid

negative space: space between solids, void or empty

Getting Started

1 **Demonstrate how to rule a 1" grid on the manila folder base.** Open the folder so its dimensions are 16" x 11". Start by making a mark every inch on the left edge, center spine, and right edge. Connect the marks with a ruler. Let students work on their grids, using your model as an example.

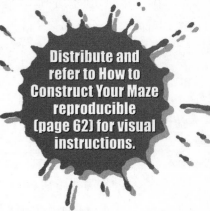

Distribute and refer to How to Construct Your Maze reproducible (page 62) for visual instructions.

2 **Create the barriers for the maze.** Have each student select twenty colored index cards, fold all the cards in half lengthwise, and cut along the fold to create forty 5" long strips. Point out that there are two kinds of barriers: straight and L shaped.

> **5" long straight barrier:** Fold strip again lengthwise, then unfold.
>
> **L-shaped barrier:** Create a 5" straight barrier.
> With a ruler, mark at 3"
> Cut at 3" mark to the crease, fold back.
> Place a drop of glue on the short 2" end, fold back onto the long 3" end.
> Hold for a few seconds until secure.

Tip: *Students should go ahead and make about 15 straight and 15 L-shaped barriers to get started.*

Let's Create!

1 **Pick one box along the perimeter of the grid for the entrance to the grid and one for the exit.**

2 **Build a retaining wall around the perimeter of the base.** Have students glue 4 L-shaped barriers into the corners and enclose the perimeter with ten straight barriers. Make sure they do not block the designated entrance and exit; they may need to trim the length of their barriers to create the openings.

3 **Design the inside of the maze.** Each student will come up with a different solution for the maze, some more complex than others. Remember that each student's process of working will be different.

Tips: **1** *Show students how the grid that they measured can be used to keep a uniform width of 1 box (1") for the passages. To do this, align the back of the barriers with the lines of the grids before gluing down.*

2 *Encourage students to play with many possible passages before gluing anything down.*

3 *While it is not necessary to have worked out the entire maze in advance, students should have an idea of how they want it to start.*

4 *Remind students to keep testing their maze by tracing a finger through the passages, checking that one solution remains open. If a passage gets closed off, cut through the index cards and create an opening 1" wide.*

5 *To create an appropriate level of challenge for more sophisticated students, encourage them to use all 40 barriers, or more if necessary. Each added barrier creates a more complex and confusing maze.*

4 **Test mazes by running a ball through them.** Check that passages are uniformly 1" wide.

Finish the Project

Students can compare their mazes and time a partner who tries to finish the maze quickly. The challenger can drop the ball inside the entrance and the maze builder can keep time. List the times for completion; the longer the maze takes, the more successful the maze. The builder of the most complex maze might win a prize.

Tip: *As an alternative to marbles, use soft pom-pom balls (available in craft stores).*

Display It!

 Display the mazes on the wall or bulletin board. Have students trace their fingers through the mazes, creating an interactive display.

Book Links

The Art of the Maze by Adrian Fisher and Georg Gester (Sterling Publishing, 2000)

Mazes and Labyrinths: Their History and Development by William Henry Matthews (Dover Publishing, 1970)

Web Links

http://www.mazemaker.com
Life-size mazes by artist Adrian Fisher

http://eluzions.com/Puzzles/Mazes/
Web site featuring kid-friendly mazes, puzzles, and activities

http://www.mazes.com
Portfolios of mazes

http://www.minotaur-websites.com/minomyth.htm
The story of Theseus and the Minotaur

⁕ This three-dimensional project stacks neatly and compactly: 24 mazes make a pile only 18" high.

Art and Language Extensions

⁕ Try building a second maze that is bigger, or join two individual mazes together.

⁕ Experiment with passages that run diagonally within the grid, and with covered tunnels as well.

⁕ Read aloud the myth of Theseus and the Minotaur. Ask students to determine whether Daedalus constructed a maze or a labyrinth to house the monster. Have them draw their own conclusions based upon the readings. Then, ask them to create a scale model of a scene from the myth, complete with figures of Theseus searching for the Minotaur in the maze.

Investigate Further

⁕ Have students research the distinction between labyrinths and mazes. Labyrinths have been used in many cultures as a form of meditation or initiation. Many medieval cathedrals had floor labyrinths for "prayer walks." Where can your students find a walk-through labyrinth near your school?

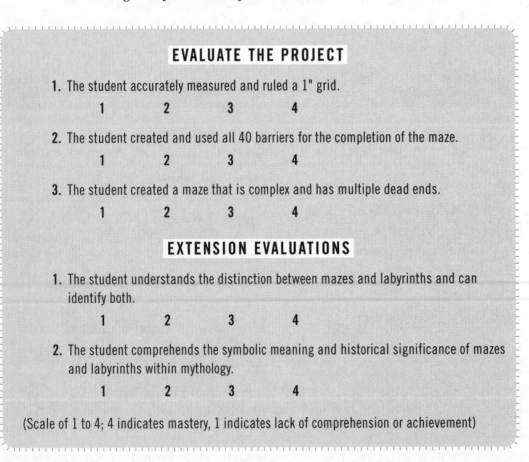

EVALUATE THE PROJECT

1. The student accurately measured and ruled a 1" grid.

    1   2   3   4

2. The student created and used all 40 barriers for the completion of the maze.

    1   2   3   4

3. The student created a maze that is complex and has multiple dead ends.

    1   2   3   4

EXTENSION EVALUATIONS

1. The student understands the distinction between mazes and labyrinths and can identify both.

    1   2   3   4

2. The student comprehends the symbolic meaning and historical significance of mazes and labyrinths within mythology.

    1   2   3   4

(Scale of 1 to 4; 4 indicates mastery, 1 indicates lack of comprehension or achievement)

Maze Planning Sheet

Use this page to create a maze. By connecting the dots in the grid with a solid line, you can show barriers and pathways. Make your perimeter a solid line with one entrance and exit.

How to Construct Your Maze

Name:_____ Class:_____ Date:_____

Rule a 1" grid onto the open-folder base.

Dimensions: 16" x 11"

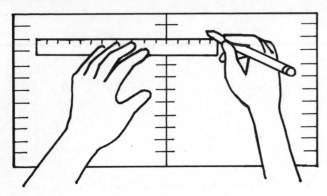
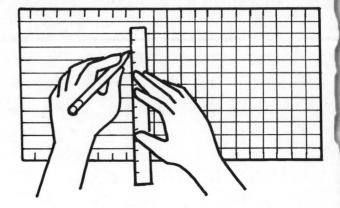

Construct 5-inch long straight barriers.

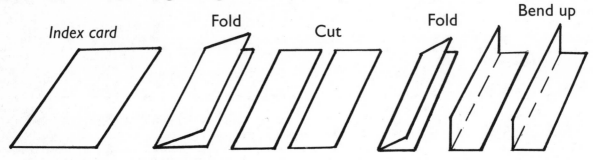

Index card   Fold   Cut   Fold   Bend up

Construct L-shaped Barriers

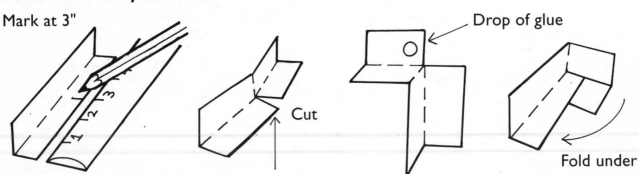

Mark at 3"   Cut   Drop of glue   Fold under

Construct Perimeter

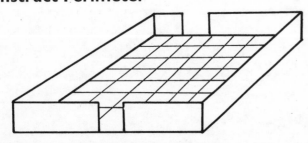

Note: Leave open an entrance and an exit. Have 15 straight and 15 L-shaped barriers pre-assembled to arrange on the grid. Experiment with placement before gluing.

Sky's the Limit: Skyscraper Contest

Design and construct a skyscraper model from paper modular units

Skyscrapers are a symbol of power, economic strength, and technological ingenuity. Challenge the class to a contest: Which team can build the tallest, most stable, and distinctive skyscraper? This project combines science, technology, and social studies within a collaborative project.

What Students Will Learn and Do

* ☀ Learn that a skyscraper is supported by an inner steel frame.

* ☀ Learn names and functions of architectural terms.

* ☀ Learn how wind stress acts upon a tall structure.

* ☀ Understand that architecture combines aesthetics and technology.

* ☀ Work together in a team project, through all phases of conceptualization, drawing, construction, and testing of the final design.

Materials

How to Design Your Skyscraper reproducible, pages 69–70

Large cardboard base, one per team

Long, rectangular boxes (such as those containing rolls of bulletin board paper), one or two per team.

5" x 8" unlined index cards (at least 100 for each team); various colors

A pack of white copy paper, pre-cut in half to the dimensions $5\frac{1}{2}" \times 8\frac{1}{2}"$

Rulers, scissors, markers, pencils, and scotch tape for each team

Large electric fan for wind test

Tips: ❶ *Index cards will form the beams, ceilings, and floors of the skyscraper. Buy colored index cards to add visual interest to the project. Students may also wish to give a function to the colors by designating one color as commercial space, one color as residential space, and so forth.*

❷ *While index cards are available in different sizes (3" x 5", 4" x 6", and 5" x 8") the largest size will form the most realistic model, as the span between the columns will be the greatest.*

Get the Class Thinking

Find out what students already know about skyscrapers. Ask them questions such as:

* How many skyscrapers can you name?

* Why do you see skyscrapers in big cities, and not in the country?

* Some sections of a city don't have big skyscrapers, while other sections do. Why do you think that's so?

* How do you think it's possible to build skyscrapers so tall?

Explain how several circumstances combine to make skyscrapers commercially necessary and physically possible: high population density in a small land area and a firm foundation, called bedrock, to build upon. The high cost of land in densely populated areas means that the best way for real estate developers to turn a profit is to build as high as they can. Skyscrapers are technologically possible because of two American inventions: steel beams and the electric elevator.

Challenge the class to a contest to create the tallest skyscraper it can by stacking paper modules (you may want to limit each team to 50 modular units to set a

Vocabulary

architecture: the art of designing structures in which people live and work

building frame: the inner steel skeleton that supports a building and gives its shape

modular units (modules): sections of a building that are pre-assembled, then connected together at the site

elevator core: the rigid "spine" of the skyscraper, made of elevator shafts that are bundled together and reinforced

column: a vertical support that bears weight

beam: a horizontal connection between columns that bears the weight of floors and ceilings

flange: a protruding rim or edge used to hold an object in place or attach it to another object

span: the distance between columns

foundation: the part of the skyscraper that goes below the surface and connects it to the Earth

piers: large "pins" that are drilled into bedrock to anchor the skyscraper

bedrock: a solid rock layer in the Earth that will not move or shift under a weight

elevation drawing: a drawing of what the building would look like as seen from the side

footprint: the perimeter of the building at ground level

realistic parameter). The paper modules will mimic steel-frame construction. The skyscrapers students build should be stable structures that will not topple over. Explain that the class will test the paper skyscrapers with a wind stress test after completion.

Post the goals for the skyscraper contest:

☀ As high as possible (Establish a minimum height of six feet.)

☀ As stable as possible against a wind force

☀ As imaginative as possible in appearance and design

Show pictures of skyscraper rooftops. Skyscrapers frequently have elaborate tops and lighting that distinguish the building's shape in a skyline.

Getting Started

1 **Divide the class into teams.** Group students into four teams of seven to eight members or make just two teams by having the boys challenge the girls.

2 **Have teams name themselves and their skyscrapers.** Teams may want to designate a "construction manager" who will oversee the construction and make sure the team follows its drawing plans.

Distribute and refer to How to Design Your Skyscraper reproducibles (pages 69–70) for visual instructions.

3 **Ask teams to draw their ideas of how they want their skyscraper to look.** Teams should also discuss the function of their building and whether it is a residential, commercial, or mixed-use building. Will there be a hotel, restaurant, or observatory at the top? Would it house a corporation's headquarters or a government agency? These decisions about the building's function will shape its final appearance. Finally, how will the team make the top look distinctive?

4 **Post the drawings.** The teams will have decided on their concepts but may modify their ideas as they build.

5 **Demonstrate how to make a paper modular unit.** You may want to make a transparency of the reproducible on page 69 so you can refer to the modular-unit diagram on the overhead projector. Each modular unit consists of 4 "columns" and 2 "beams" made from index cards.

1. To make the columns: Use the pre-cut white copy paper. Take one sheet and roll it onto a marker. The marker acts as a form for the column. Tape the rolled paper closed and push out the marker with a pencil.

2. To make the beams: Fold up a half-inch flange on either side of the index card.

3. Tape the columns to the index-card beams, criss-crossing the tape as shown in the diagram. For extra strength, add a piece of tape to the inside edge of the column.

Tip: *Although the modules are easy to construct, it is important that students do not rush, but carefully align the columns in the corners of the beams. This will prevent the modular units from warping when taped, and the columns will line up when stacked together.*

6 **Each team member should create four modular units.** This will provide the team with enough units to begin to assemble the ground floor.

Let's Create!

1 **Select a cardboard base.** Have each team write its name on their cardboard base.

2 **Arrange the elevator core and the footprint on the base of the building.** Ask students to place the rectangular packing box vertically on the cardboard base and trace its position. Then ask them to arrange the ground floor modular units on the base and trace around them to create the footprint.

3 **Tape and glue the elevator core to the base.** Have students glue the ground floor modular units into place.

4 **Assemble modular units and tape them together to create floors.** Be sure that students take care to align the modular units so that the building does not lean. Then have students tape units together by the beams to create levels and floors as shown on the reproducible.

> **Tip:** *Set a materials limit of 100 index cards (50 modular units) per team. Hold the students accountable for keeping track of their cards. How high and stable can they build within these limits?*

5 **Erect the skyscraper frame to at least the required minimum height.** A second elevator core (rectangular packing box) may need to be taped on top of the first before adding additional modules.

6 **Top it off.** Teams finish their skyscrapers with distinctive tops.

Finish the Project

Have each team subject their skyscraper to a wind test with a powerful fan. Depending on the strength of the fan, the building may topple, sway, or shift on the table if poorly built. While toppling or shifting in location is unacceptable, students may be surprised to learn that for a building to sway slightly in the wind is, in fact, normal and even necessary. A real skyscraper may sway several feet off center. Architects take wind sway into account in designing a structure.

Art and Language Extensions

❋ Ask students to add a foundation to the building. While gluing the ground floor to the base created a simple foundation, a more realistic foundation can be made by placing the entire structure onto a bake pan filled with air-dry clay. Have students duplicate the use of piers driven into bedrock by pushing nails through the first floor into the clay.

* Encourage students to add details to the frame. They can create a doorway or a main entrance area, add a plaza or community space at the ground level, use index cards to cantilever balconies jutting from the upper floors, and curve, fold, or shape index cards to add decorative elements.

* Have teams enclose the frame by creating exterior walls:
  * Use index cards taped to the columns, with windows cut out
  * Wrap the structure using clear plastic wrap to create the effect of all-glass "curtain walls"

Investigate Further

* Have the class research famous skyscrapers, such as: the Empire State Building, the Chrysler Building, the Sears Tower, the Petronas Towers in Malaysia, and the ill-fated Twin Towers. Who designed these structures? How tall are (were) they? What technological innovations did each contribute to skyscraper technology?

* Offer students the opportunity to see the "guts" of a building. Ask the school custodian to give the class a tour of the school's basement to see the H.V.A.C. system (heating, ventilating, and air conditioning) to understand how a building meets human needs.

* Challenge students to investigate, compare, and contrast various building systems (H.V.A.C., mechanical room, frame, exterior wall, foundation, elevators, waste management) to the organ systems of the human body. In what ways are building systems like human systems? Are there any two systems directly parallel in function? Compare a diagram of building systems with a diagram of the human skeletal, circulatory, digestive, respiratory, nervous, and endocrine systems.

* Have the class visit a construction site in your town or take pictures of a building under construction. Compare the photos to the models the teams built. How many architectural features in the photographs can students name?

* Ask teams to calculate the scale of their skyscrapers: If each modular unit is $5\frac{1}{2}"$ high, representing one floor (the standard height is 12' for a residential floor, 16' for a commercial floor), how many feet do the paper models represent?

Book Links

The Art of Construction: Projects and Principles for Beginning Engineers and Architects by Mario Salvadori (Chicago Review Press, 1990)

The Fantastic Cutaway Book of Giant Buildings by Jon Kirkwood (Millbrook Press, 1997)

Skyscrapers: Inside and Out by Leonard Joseph (Rosen Publishing Group, Inc. 2001)

Unbuilding by David MacCaulay (Houghton Mifflin Co., 1986)

Web Link

http://www.salvadori.org
Web site for the Salvadori Middle School Program for Architectural Design

EVALUATE THE PROJECT

1. Teams created a skyscraper from stacking and aligning paper modular units and worked from a design plan.

     1   2   3   4

2. The skyscraper has an elevator core, a defined entrance, and a distinctive top.

     1   2   3   4

3. The skyscraper passed a wind stress test without toppling over or shifting on its base.

     1   2   3   4

EXTENSION EVALUATIONS

1. Students calculated the scale of the skyscraper model and determined the height it represents in feet.

     1   2   3   4

2. Students understand and can compare the functions of building systems to the systems of the human body.

     1   2   3   4

(scale of 1 to 4; 4 indicates mastery, 1 indicates a lack of comprehension or achievement)

How to Design Your Skyscraper

Constructing a Modular Unit

Roll up the column with a marker.
Tape it and push out the marker with a pencil.

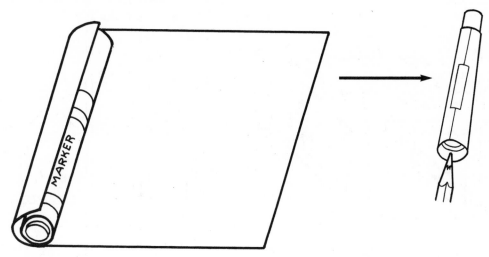

Fold up $\frac{1}{2}$ inch flanges on index cards to create the top and bottom beams of the unit.

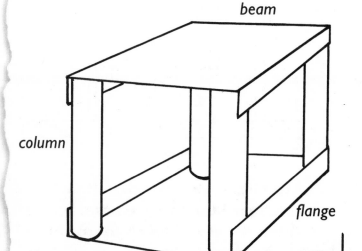

beam

column

flange

corner placement

Set a column in each corner of the unit. Align the columns in the corners carefully.

Secure the columns on the outside and inside of the modular unit with tape.

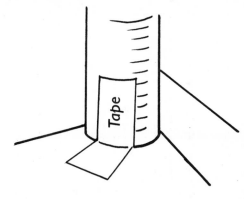

Tape

Criss-cross tape for extra support.

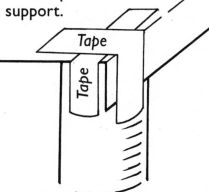

Tape

Tape

How to Design Your Skyscraper

Combining the Modular Units

Tape the modular units together, securing beams and flanges with tape at the top, sides, and bottom of each unit.

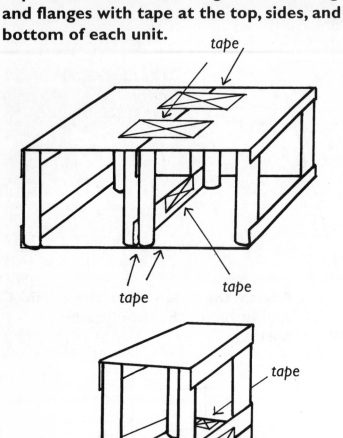

tape

tape

tape

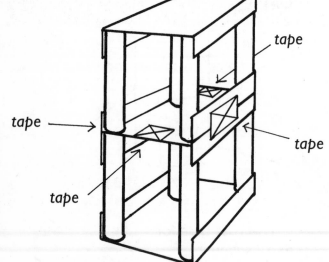

tape

tape

tape

tape

tape

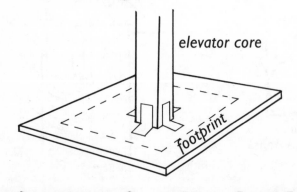

elevator core

footprint

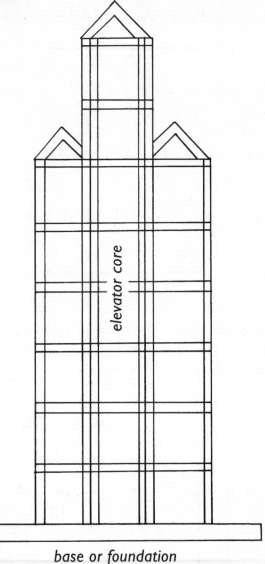

elevator core

base or foundation

Attach the elevator core (tall cardboard box) to the base. Trace the skyscraper's footprint on the base.

Follow the outline of the footprint. Tape modular units to the base and elevator core.

Finish with a unique top.

Sun Medallion Mania

Create a three-dimensional model of a sun symbol

The sun is a universal image of life, affirmation, abundance, goodness, and growth. Throughout history the sun has been worshiped as a god and appropriated as a symbol of power. Today,

images of the sun can be found on packages, sport logos, and tattoos. This project can serve as a springboard to language arts, social studies, and science concepts. It can spark investigation and comparison of sun myths and images from different cultures, as well as the study of scientific facts about the sun's composition.

What Students Will Learn and Do

- ☀ Create a three-dimensional model of a sun symbol.
- ☀ Research mythology and imagery connected with the sun.
- ☀ Create personifications for the sun by drawing faces with expressions.
- ☀ Learn how to use a right triangle to place equidistant marks on the circumference of the plate.

Materials

Expression Sketch Sheet: Sun Medallion reproducible, page 76

Sun Ray Template reproducible, page 77

Positioning Your Sun Rays: How to Position the Right Triangle, Step by Step reproducible, page 78

How to Assemble Your Sun Medallion reproducible, page 79

Paper plates, 10 $\frac{3}{4}$" in diameter, heavy weight with flat rims

Right triangles (angles measuring 30, 60, and 90 degrees)

Box of craft sticks, white glue, oaktag, pencils, markers, colored pencils or crayons.

Standard number 10 letter envelopes

Get the Class Thinking

Ask the class what they already know about the sun. What would life be like without the sun? Could there be any life on Earth at all? What feelings do you associate with the sun? Do you prefer rainy and cold days or warm and sunny days? What do you think it means to have a "sunny" personality?

Enhance students' motivation by making your discussion visual. Bring several images of the sun from different cultures and different historical periods (see Book and Web Links). Ask why so many ancient cultures made an image of the sun part of their worship. Why do students think so many images of the sun are created with a human face? Questions like these make a great lead-in to introducing the concept of personification.

Show a picture of a medallion to the class. See if students can come up with a definition. You might point out that large round medals worn around the neck have come back into fashion through hip-hop culture.

Getting Started

Sketch out ideas for medallions. Distribute the Expression Sketch Sheet: Sun Medallion reproducible. Make sure that students have seen and discussed a variety of sun images. Keep a variety of ancient and contemporary images on hand for students to refer to as they work. Students can easily create additional templates by tracing a plastic coffee can lid or small paper plate to create a circle for their sun. Encourage them to have fun with their drawings and to create a face that has a strong emotion. Finish the sketches by drawing sun rays on the circle's circumference and by adding color.

Ask students to write a sentence describing the emotion they drew for their sun face. What would this sun say to you?

Tip: *Even if you don't have time to do the three-dimensional project, these color sketches make a stunning display when presented together!*

Let's Create!

1 **Draw the face.** When students have completed a sketch, have them draw that face in pencil on the bottom side of the paper plate. Encourage students to make any revisions in pencil before reinforcing the finished drawing by tracing over the lines with a marker.

2 Create the sun rays. Photocopy and distribute the Sun Ray Template reproducible. Invite students to create their own sun ray shapes as well. Students should cut out one of the sun ray shapes, and then use the cutout as a template to trace additional rays onto oaktag or stiff poster board. Students can choose a second sun ray design and alternate the two to create a pattern. Six rays of each design, or 12 total rays, are needed to go around the plate circumference.

Have students glue one craft stick onto each sun ray, pushing the stick up to the tip of the ray so that it supports the paper shape. This step will keep the ray from getting bent!

> **Tip:** *At cleanup, store each student's sunrays and craft sticks in a standard number 10 envelope labeled with the student's name.*

3 Position the sun rays. This is a great opportunity to incorporate measurement practice with a right triangle. Have students mark twelve equidistant marks on the circumference or rim of the paper plate, following the steps below and referring to the diagrams on the reproducible.

> **Distribute and refer to Positioning Your Sun Rays: How to Position the Right Triangle, Step by Step (page 78) for visual instructions.**

a) Hold the paper plate with the thumb and forefinger with one hand, making sure that the drawn face is right side up. Mark the top of the plate on the flat rim with a vertical line. Write the word "top" next to the line.

b) Put the plate face down. Find the center of the circle. (On "Chinet" brands, this is easy; the dot on the "i" in the word "Chinet" is the center.) Mark the center.

c) Place the right triangle so that the 90-degree angle touches the center and the vertical line marked "top." (See diagram on student handout.) The bottom edge of the right triangle will touch the rim at the 3:00 position. Mark it.

d) Flip the right triangle upside down, align it, and mark at the 6:00 position.

e) Flip the right triangle, align it, and mark at the 9:00 position.

f) To mark the other eight sun ray positions, use the 30-degree angle always positioned at the center. Align the 90-degree angle along the four quadrants already marked. Flip the triangle over and keep marking.

> **Tips: ❶** *Don't have enough right triangles? Make a template on oaktag or cardboard. Any square piece of cardboard or folder can be used to create a right angle.*
>
> **❷** *Refer to the twelve markings by the time of the clock when you model this activity. Your students will instantly understand to which mark you are referring.*
>
> **❸** *Distinguishing between 30 and 60 degrees can be confusing for special needs or learning disabled students, so label these angles on the template or right triangle.*
>
> **❹** *Students who have trouble with step 3 may instead estimate the position of the two sun rays between each of the four quadrants.*

4 Assemble the model. Have students put a ring of white glue on the flat rim that has been marked. Arrange the sunrays in an alternating pattern on the marks. Refer students to the diagram on the Sun Ray Template reproducible.

After all of the rays are arranged, put another ring of white glue on top of them. Take another plate, turn it over, and cover the plate with the sun rays. Make sure that the two plates are aligned. Weigh it down with several books for at least ten minutes.

Tip: *This is a natural stopping place for the day's art activities.*

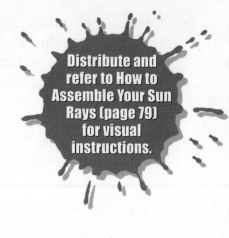

Distribute and refer to How to Assemble Your Sun Rays (page 79) for visual instructions.

Finish the Project

☀ Have students use markers, crayons, colored pencils, or paint to finish coloring the face.

☀ Ask them to decorate the medallions with foil, yarn, sequins, glitter, mosaic tiles, or wood shapes.

☀ Invite students to add dimensional elements: nose, eyebrows, large "google eyes" that jiggle (available in craft stores).

Display It!

☀ Display on shelf.

☀ Staple to bulletin board.

☀ Adhere to wall with double-stick tape.

☀ Punch out hole in sun ray, hang up by thread from light fixture.

Art and Language Extensions

☀ Because two plates are needed, most students will want to create a second image or face. Encourage them to explore a face with a contrasting emotion. As they think of antonyms, challenge students to draw these combinations:

sleepy/awake

nervous/calm

joyful/depressed

evil/angelic

☀ Ask students to write dialogues between these two contrasting faces and display the dialogues with the medallion.

☀ Have students staple other antonym pairs to the sun rays to turn the entire project into a language mobile.

Book Links

Beyond the Blue Horizon: Myths and Legends of the Sun, Moon, Stars and Planets by E.C. Krupp (Oxford University Press, 1992)

Sun Lore: Folk Tales and Sagas Around the World by Gwydion O'Hara (Llewellyn Publications, 1997)

Web Links

Punching in keywords "Sun Images in Mythology" yields numerous of web links.

Try key-wording specific gods or myths. The key words "sun images" or "sun pictures" call up links to scientific pictures of the sun. Also try:

http://ancienthistory.about.com/ Web site for information about ancient civilizations

http://www.encyberpedia.com/ Online encyclopedia for specific research on myths

☀ Instead of drawing faces, challenge students to cut or collage onto the medallion various magazine pictures of people expressing feelings. As an alternative, take two photos of each student expressing contrasting feelings and glue onto the plates.

Investigate Further

☀ Why was worship of the sun crucial to the lives of ancient peoples? How did their practices and stories differ? Students can compare and contrast traditions of worship and sun myths. Pick any two to create a pair:

Ancient Egyptian

Greek

Roman

Celtic Druid

Aztec

African

Ancient Babylonian

Native American

☀ The sun is still a compelling image found in advertising, sport logos and tattoos. Create a "sun gallery" of images found in contemporary media. Students can write about their perceptions of why the sun image was chosen to represent a brand or a team.

EVALUATE THE PROJECT

1. The student completed a sun medallion with one or two faces that express an emotion.

1   2   3   4

2. The student used a right angle to make equidistant placement of the sun rays around the circumference of the circle.

1   2   3   4

EXTENSION EVALUATIONS

1. The student understood the concept of personification and/or antonyms.

1   2   3   4

2. The student wrote a dialogue expressing contrasting emotions.

1   2   3   4

3. The student understood the importance of images of the sun in cultural and historical contexts.

1   2   3   4

(Scale of 1 to 4; 4 indicates mastery, 1 indicates lack of comprehension or achievement)

Expression Sketch Sheet: Sun Medallion

Design a sun medallion with an original expression.

Words that describe my sun medallion's expression: _____

_____

If it could talk it would say: _____

_____

Sun Ray Template

You will need to make 12 rays for your medallion. Here are sample sun rays for you to cut out and trace. Select one or more for your sun ray pattern.

To create the rays, glue a craft stick on the back of each. Place the stick near tip of ray.

Positioning Your Sun Rays: How to Position the Right Triangle, Step by Step

Carefully place the right triangle before you make a mark on the rim of the plate. The 90° and 30° angle must touch the center dot on the plate. The right triangle must touch the previous line drawn on the rim before you draw the next mark on the rim. Double check each placement before you draw!

Use the 90° angle to make the quarter circle marks at the 12 o'clock, 3 o'clock, 6 o'clock, and 9 o'clock positions.

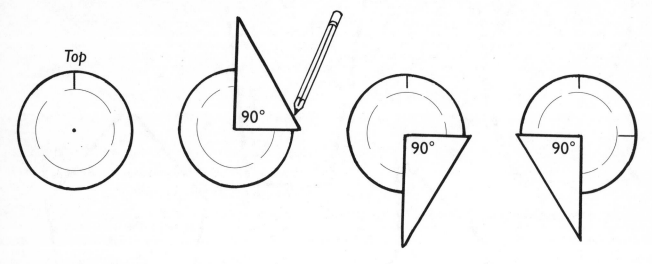

Use the 30° angle to make the marks in between.

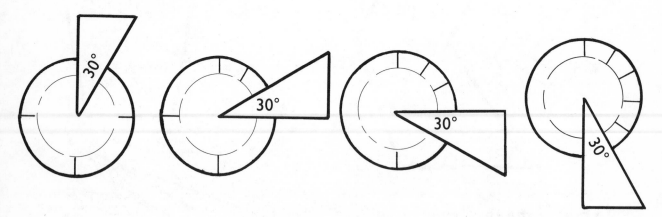

Continue marking the position of the sun rays around the plate from the six o'clock position back to the top. You should have 12 marks in all.

How to Assemble Your Sun Medallion

Glue rays to rim of plate, following marks.

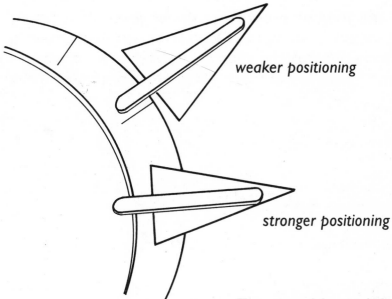

weaker positioning

stronger positioning

To assemble, weigh down the top plate with a stack of heavy books. Allow to dry for several hours.

Cover rays with glue.

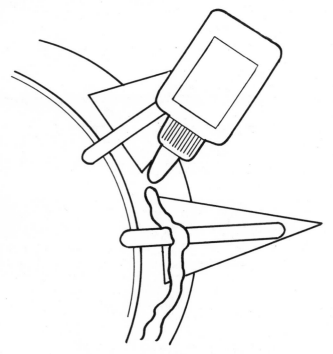

Evaluate Your Project

Project title: _____

✸ Describe your most surprising discovery about this project.

_____

_____

_____

_____

_____

✸ Describe your biggest challenge in creating this project.

_____

_____

_____

_____

_____

✸ Would you recommend this project to a friend? Why or why not?

_____

_____

_____

_____